BRINGING UP
M$NEY SMaRT KiDS

ADAM KHOO

author of the bestselling *I Am Gifted, So Are You*

KEON CHEE

author of the bestselling *Make Your Money Work For You*

BRINGING UP

MONEY SMaRT KiDS

 **Marshall Cavendish**
Editions

Illustrations by Sharon Lei

Published by Marshall Cavendish Editions
An imprint of Marshall Cavendish International
1 New Industrial Road, Singapore 536196

Other Marshall Cavendish Offices:
Marshall Cavendish International. PO Box 65829 London EC1P 1NY, UK • Marshall Cavendish Corporation. 99 White Plains Road, Tarrytown NY 10591-9001, USA • Marshall Cavendish International (Thailand) Co Ltd. 253 Asoke, 12th Flr, Sukhumvit 21 Road, Klongtoey Nua, Wattana, Bangkok 10110, Thailand • Marshall Cavendish (Malaysia) Sdn Bhd, Times Subang, Lot 46, Subang Hi-Tech Industrial Park, Batu Tiga, 40000 Shah Alam, Selangor Darul Ehsan, Malaysia.

Marshall Cavendish is a trademark of Times Publishing Limited

National Library Board, Singapore Cataloguing-in-Publication Data
Adam Khoo and Keon Chee, author.
Bringing Up Money Smart Kids / Adam Khoo and Keon Chee – Singapore : Marshall Cavendish Editions, [2015]
pages cm
ISBN : 978-981-4328-50-0 (paperback)

1. Finance. 2. Children. I. Title

DS597.215.M3
959.5054 — dc23   OCN 899252490

Printed in Singapore by Fabulous Printers Pte Ltd

To my wife, Sally Khoo,
the most dedicated mother in the world.
—ADAM

To my mother and father,
who taught me to love and laugh everyday.
—KEON

CONTENTS

FOREWORD

In a dynamic and competitive economy like Singapore, financial literacy is extremely important, although it is not easy for a layperson to master. Parents are faced with an overabundance of economic choices daily—which is the best choice for their children?

Should parents buy branded shoes when a good quality non-branded pair is available? Should they give their children an allowance or should they be paid for performing household chores? How do you help your child to be grateful for what he has when his friends and classmates seem to have more?

It is indeed a blessing that Adam and Keon have written a book based on their own experiences. *Bringing Up Money Smart Kids* gives practical guidance to all types of parents—married, divorced, rich, poor—on how to raise financially responsible children in a time of plenty.

This book also addresses areas that parents may neglect, such as teaching their children the importance of giving and sharing, how to deal with unexpected events like death and serious illnesses, and how to leave an inheritance to your children that would not destroy their desire to work and promotes family values that are important to you.

The life experiences and personal stories of these authors are invaluable, because no theory or textbook can speak louder than real life stories.

Every parent should read this book.

JAMES SIM
Past President, Financial Planning Association of Singapore

INTRODUCTION

Bringing up Money Smart Kids is written for parents and caregivers of preschoolers to teens—namely kids between the ages of five and eighteen. These parents face the challenging issue of teaching their children how to manage their money in an era where time is scarce and more money is available.

This book is written by parents for parents. Adam and Keon are wealth experts and parents themselves. They also run regular courses on money management for other children.

ADAM KHOO

Adam is the executive chairman of Adam Khoo Learning Technologies Group, one of Asia's largest training companies. A self-made millionaire at the age of 26 and financially free at 33, Adam teaches personal financial management and investing at the renowned Wealth Academy in Singapore, Malaysia, Indonesia and Vietnam.

Adam also trains students and their parents in personal development, learning and life skills. For the past 21 years, he has reached out to over 500,000 youth in seven countries. Adam's much sought-after programmes are conducted in over 120 Singapore schools, international schools around the Asian region as well as at his Adam Khoo Learning Centres. Financial literacy is an essential component of the twenty-first century learning competencies that he teaches to youth as part of their holistic education.

Adam has two daughters, Kelly (ten years old) and Samantha (eight years old). Adam is proud that his daughters have learnt the value of money. Once, Kelly was asked to pick her own birthday present at Toys R' Us. After spotting a doll that caught her eye, she looked at the price tag and said, "It's too expensive. It's not worth it." Adam could not have been more proud as a father.

What Adam hopes to achieve

It is his aim that through this book, parents will learn the importance of, and gain the knowledge on how to bring up financially responsible children. Through the course of his work, he has seen many parents spoil their children and unknowingly instil destructive financial habits in them. For example, they buy their children whatever they ask for and throw them lavish thousand-dollar birthday parties to impress their friends. Their children may score good grades and land well-paid jobs when they grow up. However, they may inevitably end up struggling financially and even get themselves into serious debt if they carry such poor overindulgent money habits into their adulthood.

Being born into a wealthy family can be both a boon as well as a bane to a child's future success—personally and financially. While being born into a privileged family has obvious advantages, it can also lead to children lacking personal drive and developing poor money habits if they are given things too easily. Like the old saying goes, 'the first generation builds the wealth, the second generation enjoys the wealth and the third generation destroys the wealth.'

If children never go through the experience of having to struggle and work hard for money, they will never develop the persistence, tenacity and self-motivation to build their own wealth and success. This is why many tycoons are now insisting that their children work at minimum wage jobs and pay for their own college education even though they can give their children an easier way out. They recognise that by helping their child in the short term, they are actually doing more harm to their children in the long term. Recently, it was reported that the son of David Beckham (the famous football star who is worth £165 million), fifteen-year-old Brooklyn Beckham has started working a weekend job at a West London coffee shop where he is paid £2.68 an hour. They encourage their children to get part-time jobs to pay their own expenses to teach them the importance of hard work and appreciate the value of money.

The best way to destroy your children's hunger for success and money values is to give them what they want.

KEON CHEE

Keon works in an estate planning company that specialises in wills, trusts and corporate services. He is a firm believer of lifelong learning for everyone. After graduating from Columbia University and working in finance for many years, he obtained a law degree from the University of London at the 'ripe' age of 53. To encourage his daughter Sarah to learn the violin, Keon started learning the piano at 39 and has passed his Grade 7 albeit after a few tries.

Sarah is 21 years old and is studying fashion merchandising and music at the University of Arizona. Keon is proud of Sarah for her thoughtfulness—even though Sarah had a music scholarship, she insisted on working as a waitress in the school cafeteria and as a salesgirl at Macy's while studying to pay for her own expenses.

What Keon hopes to achieve

Kids need to learn that having sufficient money is necessary for a comfortable life. Living in fear of being broke all the time can be miserable. There are important money management lessons like saving, investing and borrowing that everyone, including parents, can master to become financially successful. Secondly, kids need to practise gratitude each and every day, whether it is in giving or in receiving. Being grateful is a goal higher than achieving a comfortable life. It makes for a happy and fulfilling life.

WRITTEN IN A SIMPLE, PRACTICAL WAY

No one likes to hang around naggy people, not even naggy people. They repeat themselves and are tiring to listen to. We want to give you simple advice that works and does not require tons of effort to implement. Time-constrained parents want to be able to do something right away. This book will equip you with simple but important money management habits that you can apply to help your child to achieve financial success in their future.

CHAPTER 1
MORE THAN JUST MONEY

PARENTS NEED MORE GUIDANCE

Children today have more money of their own and the added pressure to spend it than in all of history. Most parents work, and with mounting chores and responsibilities are often stretched for time. Living in a day and age where time is scarce and money is not, parents need more guidance than ever on how to teach their children to handle their money in a responsible manner.

POOR SPENDING HABITS CAN BE DISASTROUS

Money is an essential tool but it can also confuse and hurt. It is earned to feed and clothe, or to save or invest for future needs. But many children today—from both wealthy or middle class families— grow up not having to worry about money, not having to support their parents or save for college. They develop huge appetites for spending and bring these habits into their adult lives, sometimes with disastrous consequences. These children then grow into adults who are incapable of managing their money.

Many parents have poor money habits too. They overspend on their children and work till their senior years to send their children to college, neglecting their own retirement needs. You do not want to be one of the thousands reaching their retirement years who cannot afford to retire. And you do not want to be one those hapless parents whose children develop self-defeating lifestyles because they didn't pick up good money habits from a young age.

DO YOU OVERSPEND ON YOUR CHILDREN?

Let's start with you. Are you allowing your children to overspend?

* Do you gripe about your child's mobile phone bills but pay them anyway?
* Does your son regularly drink gourmet hot chocolate that is many times more costly than a cup of Milo?
* Are there half a dozen dresses that your daughter owns that she has not worn?

You need to be putting at least 10 to 20 percent of your income into a retirement plan. If you are nowhere close, you may be spending too much on your family and child-related expenses and too little on yourself.

Spending less on your kids is not a crime

Spending less on your children is not a crime. You are not being cheap. It's plain smart:

* You can spend sparingly on infant and preschool items because kids at that age outgrow things very quickly.
* You can find good and lightly-used toys and books at low prices on websites like eBay, Gumtree and Locanto.
* You can simply say "no" to unscheduled purchases.

When you consciously spend less, prepare yourself for some whining. It can be hard to say no to kids but don't waver. In the end, your kids will thank you for the lessons learnt while you work your way to a financially comfortable retirement.

Be confident about being a good money teacher

Are you a good money teacher? You must feel confident of yourself. Confidence is the foundation of personal success. People (your children included) have a natural tendency to trust you more when you are confident. Would you see a doctor who doubts his own abilities? Would your kids look to you as a money manager if you are not confident?

If you are not confident, this is an opportunity for you to learn along with your children. No matter how much money you have, you need to be confident about managing money.

Start with a seriously positive attitude

> *"The greatest discovery of all time is that a person can change his future by merely changing his attitude."*
> —OPRAH WINFREY

...think positive ...
think positive ...
think positive

Whether it's about money or your job, avoid negative thinking. Negative thinking is powerful and detrimental to our selves, our families and our marriages. It sucks the life right out of us. If you frequently talk about how boring your job is, your children will not look forward to working in the future. So you have to live proactively and your children will learn from you.

In the UK, the education minister Elizabeth Truss warned that parents who say "I cannot do maths" are harming their children and Britain's long-term economic prospects. She said that a damaging anti-maths culture must be reversed to stop the country and its students from slipping further behind their international rivals. She condemned adults who chuckle at their own ineptitude at basic arithmetic, claiming they are giving their children a dangerous message that maths is unimportant.[1]

1　"Parents who say 'I can't do maths' are harming pupils and Britain's economic prospects, minister warns," *The Daily Mail*, 3 January 2014.

Being positive is easier than you think. If you don't have enough money for a sought-after vacation, talk about the highlights of the modestly-priced vacation you signed up for or say that when you have more spare money the next time round, the family will get to go for a longer vacation.

Quiz

Before we leave this chapter, let's see how well you handle some typical questions that children ask. If you find these questions tough, you're not alone. That's because kids have a gift for getting into situations that challenge the best of us. Take the test and see how you score.

1. **Your ten-year-old has been saving his school allowance for a Teksta T-Rex that walks sideways and burps. He's saved enough and he now wants to buy it. You:**
   a. Allow him to buy it.
   b. Tell him he can't touch his savings.
   c. Say no and offer him a talking dictionary.
   d. Buy it for him so he can keep his savings.

   (a) 3 (b) 1 (c) 0 (d) 0
   If your child has been saving for this toy, then letting him buy it is just reward for his efforts. Of course the toy should be a planned purchase, something he had been saving up for the past two months or so. The worst thing to do is to stop him from buying the toy when you and he had planned beforehand that he would be allowed to.

2. **You usually pay $40 for jeans for your son. Now he wants $120 for a branded version. You:**
   a. Flatly say the $120 pair is out of the question.
   b. Give him $40 and let him come up with the rest.
   c. Buy him the branded jeans because it's time to give him a nice pair.
   d. Say you will buy him a $40 pair or he'll just have to keep wearing his old jeans.

(a) 1 (b) 3 (c) 1 (d) 2
This would be a good lesson to teach the difference between needs and wants. For a young child, a pair of $40 jeans is plainly adequate if that is the general price for a good and comfortable pair of jeans. If he really wants the $120 pair, then he has to use his own savings or save for it. You may also consider flatly refusing to allow him to buy the $120 jeans even if he has the money. There is a limit on which a young person should spend on basic goods like a pair of jeans.

3. **Your twelve-year-old gets an allowance for mopping the floor. She recently stopped mopping. You:**
   a. Stop the allowance to punish her.
   b. Get a part-time maid to mop the floor.
   c. Continue the allowance to keep your side of the deal.
   d. Make the household chore a separate issue from the allowance.

(a) 0 (b) 0 (c) 0 (d) 3
Kids need a regular income in the form of an allowance to teach them essential money skills—saving, spending and sharing. If an allowance is tied to chores and those chores are not performed, then your child would be receiving an irregular allowance. As adults, we know that an irregular salary makes it more challenging to plan. What's more for kids?

4. **You are at the toy store with your daughter and she's pleading for a Cayla doll, an internet-connected doll that can answer questions using Google software. You:**
   a. Buy it to avoid a scene.
   b. Buy it but tell her you'll be deducting her allowance for it.
   c. Don't buy it and tell her next time she has to use her own savings.
   d. Ask her to play with the doll at her cousin's home to see if she really likes it.

(a) 0 (b) 0 (c) 3 (d) 3
You should not buy the doll if it is an unscheduled purchase. She should be encouraged to save for it if it takes no more than about two months to do so. Just to be sure, have her play with the doll to see if her interest is sustained.

5. **Your eight-year-old Ellen loses the $20 Grandma gave her for school. You:**
   a. Tell Ellen to ask Grandma nicely for another $20.
   b. Tell Ellen she should have been more careful.
   c. Let her do extra house chores for a week to earn $20.
   d. Tell her she should have put the money in her piggy bank.

(a) 0 (b) 3 (c) 1 (d) 1
You receive a $10,000 bonus from your company and you go to the casino to bet. You lose every cent. You realise that you should have been more careful. This is the same lesson that Ellen must learn. There is no way for her to get another $20 and Grandma should be told not to make the same gift twice. Ellen could work extra chores but that could have a negative spillover effect to her homework time and her normal household chores. Best that she learns to be careful from now on.

6. **After telling Samuel he absolutely cannot have the latest Sony PlayStation, Grandpa suddenly shows up with one for him. You:**
   a. Tell Grandpa Samuel can't accept the gift.
   b. Accept the gift and keep it unopened till Samuel's birthday.
   c. Give the console away to teach both Grandpa and Samuel a lesson.
   d. Accept the gift but tell him to discuss with you before buying expensive gifts for the kids.

(a) 1 (b) 2 (c) 0 (d) 3
Grandparents are wealthier today than ever before and they are notorious for spoiling their grandchildren. They give gifts at unexpected times and cannot wait for special occasions because spoiling the grandkids is a time-honoured tradition of every grandparent. You have to step in to 'discipline' Grandma and Grandpa. Tell them your kids should not receive anything expensive unless you have approved of the gift. And if they did, keep it unopened until an occasion such as Christmas, your child's birthday or when he receives good grades in school.

7. **Uncle Charlie gives nine-year-old Eileen $100 when she visited him. You:**
   a. Let her spend it as she wishes. It's a gift.
   b. Deposit the money into her piggy bank.
   c. Let her spend $20 and tell her to save the rest in her long-term savings account.
   d. Tell Uncle Charlie not to give such a large sum to Eileen.

(a) 0 (b) 1 (c) 2 (d) 3

If Uncle Charlie had given just $10 or $20, then it would be alright for Eileen to spend the gift as she wishes. But $100 is a lot of money for a nine-year-old, especially when it's an unscheduled gift. Giving a child $100 is like an adult winning the lottery. Studies show that people who do not work for the money and who suddenly receive a windfall tend to swing from one extreme of joy and excitement to emptiness and even despair.[2] Uncle Charlie needs to fall in line with your wishes. If Eileen does receive a large gift, insist that a large part of it goes towards her savings.

8. **David, your seven-year-old, usually gets too many presents on his birthday that he gets bored after opening a few gifts. You:**

    a. Give the remaining gifts to charity.

    b. Keep the remaining gifts to open another time.

    c. Open the rest of the presents to complete the task.

    d. Open a kids savings account and tell your relatives to contribute to it for his college tuition.

(a) 0 (b) 2 (c) 1 (d) 3

If you love to eat shrimp and you go to an all-you-can-eat shrimp buffet, you know that after gouging on fifty shrimp, the ones afterwards don't taste as good anymore. So if your kid receives ten presents, let him open five first and then open one every Sunday for the next five Sundays. Or better still, open a kids savings account for college. Encourage his relatives and friends to contribute to the account. Any sort of savings for college will help your kids learn about postponing instant gratification.

---

2   Robert Pagliarini, "Why playing the lottery is a good investment", *Forbes*, 17 December 2013, www.forbes.com/sites/robertpagliarini/2013/09/27/why-lottery-winners-crash-after-a-big-win/

9. **You bring four-year-old Cindy to the candy store and she wants all the chocolate she can put into the basket. You:**
   a. Let her choose one item.
   b. Leave the store and return home.
   c. Buy what she wants to avoid a scene.
   d. Put on your ear plugs and let her scream.

(a) 3 (b) 2 (c) 0 (d) 2

Tantrums aren't fun for parents, particularly during an outing or a trip to the store. If your kid cannot calm himself in public, you may need to leave the area to give them an opportunity to calm down. When you give in to her demands, she learns that the behaviour can be used as a tool for manipulation. Let her have a choice and be firm about it. Just one piece of chocolate and no more.

10. **Matthew, your five-year-old, asks what would happen to him if Mummy and Daddy died. You tell him:**
    a. You won't die (he's too young to understand death).
    b. He would live with Aunt Mary (your will specifies Aunt Mary as guardian).
    c. Someone in the family would look after him (you and your spouse are young and feel it's too early to discuss this matter).
    d. You would speak to his favourite Aunt Mary about her looking after him (you and your spouse will appoint Aunt Mary as guardian in your wills if she agrees).

(a) 1 (b) 2 (c) 1 (d) 3
Up to three years of age, kids have no understanding of death. Up to six years, they believe death is reversible, like going to sleep and waking up. Kids begin to understand the finality of death between the ages of six and nine.[3] Parents need to prepare for the possibility of both parents passing away when the kids are still young. Appointing a guardian that parents agree on is a way to ensure your kids are looked after by someone you trust when you are no longer around.

Here's how you did:

0–10   Keep this up and your kids will still be staying with you when they are 35.

11–25   Not bad but you still have some way to go.

26–30   You and your kids are on the right track. Use this book to sharpen your money-smart skills.

---

3   "Children's understanding of death", hospicenet, https://www.hospicenet.org/html/understand.html; Virginia Hughes, "When do kids understand death?", *National Geographic*, 26 July 2013, http://phenomena.nationalgeographic.com/2013/07/26/when-do-kids-understand-death/

CHAPTER 2
ALLOWANCE

With my allowance, I control what I spend. I feel independent as I don't have to rely on Daddy all the time.

ALLOWANCE + Other income =
Saving + Spending + Sharing

WHY GIVE AN ALLOWANCE?

Giving your child $0.50 a day regularly is giving an allowance. It is a fixed amount of money that he is to receive on a regular basis, with the understanding that he will pay for certain agreed-on expenses. Having a regular income is the only way children can learn to manage money. By practising with their own money, they get to try out concepts—saving for a rainy day, making spending choices and sharing with others. Giving kids an allowance:

- *Allows them to make mistakes when the cost is minimal.* Sort of like learning to drive in an empty parking lot. It is far better to make a poor choice as a kid by buying a $10 toy Ferrari than when as an adult to pay $500,000 for a real one when his pay cheque cannot cover the monthly payments.
- *Forces them to think about how much things cost, and to make spending choices between the many things they want.* If your ten-year-old cannot go to the movies with his best friend because he ran down his allowance buying game credits, he would be more careful when he gets his next allowance.
- *Gives them greater appreciation for the things they buy as they are using their own money.* Think about how often you gratefully accept goodie-bag freebies like pens and notepads only to toss them out later because you had no use for them in the first place.

When to start giving an allowance?

The best time is when your child begins to understand that money can buy him things he wants. This usually starts when he begins primary school or around six years of age. That's when they not only spend money in school but also learn about what a dollar can buy, how many cents make up a dollar and who is on the $10 note. Even if your child is over nine years old, it's never too late to start.

What does the allowance pay for?

Before your kid spends his entire allowance on toys and candy, tell him exactly what he is expected to pay for. This forces him to plan his spending. You should not tell him what to buy but you can say that his allowance is to be used for three general areas.[4] For example for every dollar of allowance:

- Spend $0.70 on regular items like food, drinks and snacks.
- Save $0.20 for irregular items like electronics and branded sneakers.
- Share $0.10 on charitable donations, and birthday presents for family and friends.

If you want something tried and tested, try the award-winning Moonjar Moneybox. It is a set of three durable moneyboxes with removable acrylic lids that teach children to save, spend and share.

---

4   For more information, see www.threejars.com/about-us/users-love

---

Create your own allowance boxes

---

1. Find three empty containers with lids, such as peanut butter jars.
2. Decorate each simply and clearly mark them for Saving, Spending and Sharing.
3. Create an opening by making a slot in the top of each container large enough to let money in, but small enough that it will not spill out.

How much allowance to give?

Fixing an allowance should be based on matching their needs. Three main considerations for you are:

- *Your child's age.* The older your child, the larger the allowance.
- *Your family income.* Be realistic about how much your family can afford to allocate to allowances.
- *What the allowance is supposed to cover.* If you expect your child to buy lunch from his allowance, then the money given each week must be sufficient. If you supplement the allowance with lunch money, then a less generous allowance is in order.

What the allowance pays for is clearly the main factor behind deciding how much to give. Sit down with your child to make a list of everything they are expected to pay for. The total required becomes their allowance. This solves the conflicts that come up in toy stores or when they go to the movies.

Please let Dad win the lottery so that he can afford to increase my allowance...

Adam says

My daughters are still young (eight and ten), so my wife and I give them a fixed allowance of $1.50 a day. They are advised on how much to spend, save and share. They are required to keep track on what they spend on every day and report to us at the end of the day. Once, my daughter spent her entire daily allowance on chocolates and sweet drinks and had skipped lunch, so she faced the consequences of getting no allowance for three days. We packed sandwiches for her for the days her allowance privileges were temporarily suspended. That's how my wife and I teach them about the consequences of making poor money choices.

Should I tie the allowance to chores?

Do you believe your kids have certain amount of responsibilities around the house just because they are members of the family? We do.

But that allowance should not be tied to chores. If allowance is tied to chores and those chores were not performed, then there would be no allowance for that week. But it's not possible to learn how to manage money without a regular income. If your child does not receive a regular allowance, it will mess up your plans to teach them about saving, spending and sharing.

In fact, if those chores are not performed, taking away some privileges would be more appropriate than deducting from their allowance. Children should understand that doing chores is part of being a family member. Since Mum and Dad do not get paid for doing family chores—why should they?

If you believe that allowance should be tied to chores

Some parents feel that an allowance is like an adult's pay cheque. It is money your kids receive for doing a few chores. If you are one of them then here's how you can keep track.

Keep a chart of chores on the refrigerator as a reminder. Have your child initial the chart after each job done (or for you to put a big gold star if your child is around preschool age).

I kept having this recurring nightmare. Everyone was doing housework and everyone was ... happy!

To Do	M	T	W	T	F	S	T
Take out rubbish	✓	✓	✓	✓	✓	XX	✓
Set table	✓	✓	✓	✓	✓	✓	XX
Clear table	✓	✓	XX	XX	✓	✓	✓
Feed Garfield	✓	✓	✓	XX	✓	✓	✓
Allowance	$ 1.00	$ 1.00	$ 0.75	$ 0.50	$ 1.00	$ 0.75	$ 0.75

Could giving an allowance be bad?

Professor Lewis Mandell thinks so. The award winning educator and economist studied more than fifty years' worth of allowance research.[5] He concludes that kids who receive a regular, unconditional allowance tend to think far less about money in general. He adds that those children appear more likely to grow up to be slackers since they do not associate work with money.

Some parents skip regular allowances altogether, which isn't necessarily a bad thing. According to Mandell, children who have to ask their parents for money each time they need it, whether it's for clothes or lunch, tend to fare better with money later in life. Perhaps this is because they are forced to think about what the money is being used for.

Review the allowance amount every year

Like adults, kids are always hoping for a raise. They may be asking for extra to spend on wants or they could be having trouble meeting their needs.

Review your child's expenses at least twice a year. Try not to decrease his allowance if he is reducing his expenses to save.

---

5   For more information, see http://lewismandell.com/child_allowances_-_beneficial_or_harmful

If you have to decrease his allowance due to financial hardship, explain this to your child and try to get his support beforehand.

As your child gets older, the basic allowance should cover more expenses. By the time your child reaches his teens, you should include a separate allowance for clothing. Giving a fixed and reasonable amount to spend on clothing provides him with another opportunity to make financial choices.

Adam says

I was privileged to be born into a wealthy family where my father and uncles were living in bungalows, driving expensive cars and earning million-dollar incomes.

I saw the immense financial freedom and security they enjoyed and it opened my mind to the possibilities of what was achievable. For my family, it was not uncommon for someone to make a million dollars a year in personal income and so it instilled my belief early in life that it was indeed possible to go from zero to hero. After all, my father and his brothers all started with absolutely nothing.

However, the greater privilege I had was that although my father was wealthy, he intentionally gave me nothing ... but love, food and educational support. He saw many kids from privileged backgrounds, who received all the financial benefits turning out spoilt and messed up. So he believed that 'you have to be cruel to be kind' and went the other extreme.

Even though we lived in a bungalow and had four country club memberships, I got less pocket money than my schoolmates. While many of my friends had lots left over for snacks, marbles and card games, my father only gave me enough for a bowl of noodles and a drink. When he gave me $2 to buy something worth $1.50, he would ensure that I returned the change.

Sometimes I felt very deprived and thought my father was a real Scrooge. But it was precisely the way he brought me up that became a blessing in disguise. It laid the foundation to my true wealth education, which was to be hungry for wealth and success.

My father believed that if a parent gave his child everything, he would kill the child's hunger for success. He knew that hunger was a key motivator and the only way to make me hungry was to deprive me. Whenever I asked him for something, his would reply predictably, "Why should I buy it for you? Buy it yourself!" So, I learnt that nobody owed me a living early on in my life.

As a result, I started to do part-time work at fourteen, going to houses to sell stationery. At fifteen, I started a small mobile disco company and became a part-time magician. The money I made from weekend gigs was used to fund my computer game, music CD and comic book collections. By the time I graduated from university at twenty-four, I had ten years of working experience in over six jobs. This gave me a huge advantage over many of my peers who graduated with the same degree but lacked the real world experience and street smarts to make and manage money. The fact that I had to earn my own money even as a student taught me to be frugal. It further stressed the importance of saving and investing for the future.

This is why I insist that my own children get vacation jobs as teenagers and pay for their own college tuition (I would give them an interest-free loan though). Only then can they truly appreciate the value of their education.

Quiz

1. **Your four-year-old Max says of his sister, "Penny has an allowance, so why can't I?" You:**

   a. Give Max $0.50 so he doesn't feel left out.

   b. Stop Penny's allowance to even things out.

   c. Tell Max that Penny is ten years old and she needs to pay for her lunches.

   d. Ignore Max as he doesn't really understand what an allowance is.

(a) 3 (b) 0 (c) 1 (d) 0

At that young age, Max has not yet experienced the need to have money to spend on things that he wants. Everything he needs is bought for him by his parents. Giving him an allowance would probably be pointless as he wouldn't know what to do with it except to roll it on the floor like a toy. Ignoring Max would be cause for unnecessary sibling rivalry.

2. **Your nine-year-old Nancy says, "My classmate Cathy gets $50, which is twice of what I get. Why?" You:**
   a. Explain that Cathy's parents are richer.
   b. Raise Nancy's allowance to match Cathy's.
   c. Give Nancy extra money now and again to make up for the difference.
   d. Tell Nancy her allowance is based on what has been planned and stick to it.

(a) 1 (b) 0 (c) 1 (d) 3
Kids compare themselves with their classmates throughout school—starting from primary school all the way to university. Kids compare everything—from allowances and snacks to the latest smart phones and laptops. The only way to stop all the nonsensical comparing is to go back to the basics—that her allowance is based on what her needs are. Then explain that Cathy probably has to use her allowance to pay for expenses that Nancy does not have to pay for.

3. **Yasmin wants a pair of $120 New Balance running shoes for school practice. The price is way over the $50 you would normally pay for her shoes. If she saved, she would take six months or more. You:**
   a. Buy the shoes for her since it's for a school activity.
   b. Let her do extra chores around the house to earn money.
   c. Tell her that she cannot have the shoes as it's over the limit.
   d. Loan her the money and have her repay with her allowance.

(a) 0 (b) 3 (c) 1 (d) 2
Paying for extra chores is quite all right especially if the child is after a big ticket item. Just make sure that the chores are above what is usually expected of them and that the money earned goes

directly into saving for that particular purchase. The lesson is: I can work harder for the special things I want. For example, you might get her to scan your old photos into your computer over the next two weeks and put $60 towards the shoe purchase. If Yasmin is really keen on the shoes, you could make an exception by loaning her the money but you must have her repay the loan. This would be similar to saving to purchase the shoes except that she is receiving the shoes today.

4. **Patrick received straight As for his mid-term exams. He's hoping for a bonus. You:**
   a. Pay him a bonus that he can spend any way he wants.
   b. Don't pay him any extra because it's like giving a bribe.
   c. Deposit a bonus amount into his college fund.
   d. Pay him a bonus but he must use the money to take his friends out for ice cream.

(a) 2 (b) 2 (c) 2 (d) 3
Parents are usually split on this one. Some say it's like giving a bribe. Kids must value education. Giving bribes is tainting that value and they will expect to be bribed to achieve good grades in future. It works even less effectively for high-achieving students. Or worse still, kids who are not high achievers may become more inconsistent. If they get a poor grade, they figure that they're not going to get the reward and give up trying to improve in school.

Paying for good grades does work for other parents. They want to recognise hard work or a job well done especially in important situations such as a mid-year exam. Kids could be told that the rewards can only be used towards certain payments such as taking their friends for an ice cream or putting 20 percent into the savings jar. Such rewards make them feel happy as they feel their parents are proud of them.

5. **Johnny usually takes the trash out at night but has not done so for the past three nights. You:**
   a. Deduct an amount from his allowance.
   b. Tell his sister Clare to take the trash out instead.
   c. Stop his TV time until he continues to take the trash out.
   d. Sit down with him to explain his responsibilities as a family member.

(a) 0 (b) 1 (c) 3 (d) 3

Allowance is not a control device. Unless the allowance is tied to specific paid chores, you should avoid threatening to withhold payment. If the allowance is related to work, indicate in writing that the allowance may be withheld if the job isn't completed.

6. **Diana gets a weekly allowance every Sunday but usually runs out of money by Wednesday. You:**
   a. Raise her allowance amount.
   b. Ask her to explain what she spends on.
   c. Revisit with her again the expenses her allowance is meant to cover.
   d. Refuse to give her any more allowance until Sunday.

(a) 0 (b) 2 (c) 3 (d) 1

Some parents require their child to account for how the money was used. You can ask your child to record her purchases in a notebook. This will help to prepare her to handle larger sums and manage a cheque book. As a rule, you should avoid questioning your child's purchasing decisions. However, you may want to offer helpful advice on how the money can be spent more productively.

7. **Matthew gets a weekly allowance. At the end of the week, he has an extra $5 after spending, saving and sharing. You:**
    a. Reduce his allowance by $5 as he may be getting too much.
    b. Encourage him to save the $5.
    c. Let him spend the $5 in any way he wishes.
    d. Find out if he's skipping on necessary expenses like food and snacks.

(a) 1 (b) 3 (c) 3 (d) 3

After putting aside money for saving and sharing, Matthew gets to spend the remainder. If he ends the week with $5 more, he could be spending less than planned in order to save more. Let him continue saving for whatever items he has in mind. Reducing his allowance would be like punishing him for making extra efforts to save. Find out if the allowance needs to be tweaked by going through his needs again with him. It may also be that Matthew is skipping essentials such as food, which should never be skipped.

8. **Sandra's allowance includes spending for movies and movie snacks. You take the whole family out for a movie. You:**
    a. Make Sandra pay for her own movie ticket.
    b. Pay half of the ticket and snacks for Sandra.
    c. Pay for Sandra's ticket but she pays for her own snacks.
    d. Pay for Sandra's ticket and snacks since it's a family gathering.

(a) 1 (b) 3 (c) 3 (d) 2

It's quite common for an item that is meant to be paid for with a kid's allowance to be paid for by his parents. For example, $10 is budgeted in his allowance for a movie and snacks with his friend, but later the whole family goes to the movies together. Making Sandra pay her own way entirely would make her feel *like she's being treated differently from the rest of the family. A good compromise is to share—Sandra could pay for her snacks or for half the ticket and snacks.*

9. **Ben's allowance includes money for gifts. It is his friend Ivy's birthday party and Ben has run out of money. You:**
   a. Tell Ben to go without a present.
   b. Give Ben money to buy a present.
   c. Tell Ben to give something that belongs to him.
   d. Have Ben make a card with a promise to buy a gift in the future.

(a) 1 (b) 0 (c) 3 (d) 3
Ivy is meant to receive a birthday present because it's her birthday and she's thrown a party. In the same way, Ben would be upset if it's his birthday party and some of his friends turned up empty-handed. Ben should give something. It could be something he currently owns that is in good condition and he is willing to give away or he should make good the gift in the future when he has saved up enough to buy a gift even if it's late.

SUMMARY

Your child's allowance should not be tied to chores. Each child should understand why she is receiving an allowance and what expenses it is supposed to cover. If you have decided to pay an allowance to your children because they are members of the family, tell them so. Remind them of the responsibilities they have as members of the family.

Once you set an amount for the allowance, pay on time. Paying on time teaches your children the value of honouring one's obligations. Never miss a payday. Make the allowance as dependable as you expect your own pay cheque to be—a regular amount on the same day each week.

CHAPTER 3
BUDGETING

BUDGETING—BEFORE YOU SAVE, SPEND OR SHARE

Soon after your child starts to receive and manage his allowance, he should learn to put together a budget. Budgeting is making sure that you're not spending more than you're bringing in. Just like running on a treadmill is a programme to keep fit, budgeting is a programme for planning to spend, save and share. It is an important component of financial success for you and your child. It will help your child to spend his money carefully for school expenses, save for toys and share a portion for good causes.

Kids (and adults) usually do not like budgeting

Be warned—telling your kids to do up a budget is like asking them to eat two helpings of broccoli in a buffet before hitting the ice cream and the fries. Even to adults, the word budgeting commonly evokes fear, stress and unhappiness. They think of budgeting as depriving themselves of fun and what they want, and they avoid it like they do the treadmill.

I don't like visiting the dentist. But it still beats doing up a budget.

Yet we all know it is important to draw up a budget. So let's go through the basics to learn how to budget. We start by filling in an Income and Expenses Worksheet. In the following exercise, your child will also learn the difference between needs and wants.

Fill in a weekly Income and Expenses Worksheet

Have your child create a weekly budget on a piece of paper. Let her fill in where her income comes from and what she has to spend on. Give her complete freedom to fill in anything else she wants, which can range from crayons to milkshakes.

Weekly Income and Expenses Worksheet

Where will my income come from?		What will I spend on?	
My allowance	$50	Lunch at school	$25
Cleaning the car	$5	Movies	$15
Gifts	$5	Bus fare	$10
Total	$60		
		How much will I Save?	
		Piggy bank	$10
		What will I Share?	
		Church	$5
		Charity	$5
		Total	$70

Looks like your child would benefit from learning the difference between needs and wants.

Adam says

It is very important for children to develop the skill of knowing how to make smart choices about how to spend their money. They need to learn the difference between needs and wants and understand that trade-offs must be made between short-term gratification and long-term rewards.

When my wife and I bring our children out to shop we always ask them, "You have a budget of $xx to spend. Would you like to spend it on this toy or save the money so that you can buy a nicer toy a few weeks or months later?" This teaches them the importance of delayed gratification. Children who have learnt the skill of delaying gratification grow up to become better students and more successful, better-adjusted, happier adults—as shown by the Marshmallow Experiment.

The Stanford Marshmallow Experiment was a series of studies on delayed gratification in the late sixties and early seventies led by psychologist Walter Mischel, then a professor at Stanford University. In those studies, a child was offered a choice between one small reward (sometimes a marshmallow, but often a cookie or a pretzel) provided immediately or two small rewards if he waited until the tester returned (after an absence of approximately fifteen minutes). In follow-up studies, the researchers found that children who were able to wait longer for the preferred rewards tended to have better life outcomes, as measured by SAT scores, educational attainment, body mass index (BMI) and other life measures.

NEEDS VERSUS WANTS

Needs are things that we truly cannot be without, such as:

- Nutritious food
- A place to live
- A good pair of shoes
- Transportation

Wants are things you would like to have, but if you don't, you'll still survive (in fact, you'll be just fine). Like:

- Designer jeans
- Ice cream
- Video games
- Latest iPhone

Wants can be postponed and they can be planned. There are times when wants become needs. When a child is a toddler, having a computer to play games on is a want. But when he turns nine and some homework requires word processing, a computer may become a need.

Keon says

When Sarah arrived, I did exactly what a new Dad does: I spoilt her. I gave her toys, candy, popsicles and anything she asked for just to make her happy. By the time she turned eight, she had turned into an out-of-control consumer.

Her mother said it was me who was out of control and that I needed to be disciplined. She said to Sarah, "Here's your weekly allowance for toys, stickers and candy. Spend it any way you want but if you finish it, you won't have any more for the rest of the week."

Sure enough, Sarah spent most of her allowance on Pokemon cards the first two weeks. I wanted to bail her out especially when she whined and shed a few tears. Sarah missed out on her favourite candy and popsicles during those initial weeks.

Then at the start of week four, she suddenly became stingy. After setting aside 10 percent each for saving and sharing, she would buy just a few Pokemon cards and she stopped. She also stopped buying candy.

Over the months, Sarah found balance—she learnt not to overspend while not becoming too tight-fisted. And she has carried this important lesson through to her young adult years.

OPPORTUNITY COST

Kids realise that budgeting means having to make spending and saving choices and that some things have to be given up because they choose to do something else. This is called opportunity cost.

For example, if your child wants to go to the movies, the opportunity cost is that she could have spent the money on food, saved it or paid for some other activity instead.

Now that you have explained the difference between needs, wants and the meaning of opportunity cost to your child, help your child to fill in his Weekly Income and Expenses Worksheet again. Start with the Income column first. Total up the Income items, then fill in the Expenses items. Before putting in any items for Spending, allocate the agreed-on amount for Saving and Sharing, say 10 percent each. The total expenses should equal the total of the Income column.

Then during the week, have your child keep track of how much was actually spent.

Weekly Income and Expenses Worksheet

Where will my income come from?		What will I spend on?		How much was spent?
My allowance	$50			
Cleaning the car	$5			
Gifts	$5			
Total	$60			
		How much will I Save?	$6 (10%)	
		What will I Share?	$6 (10%)	
		Total	$60	

BUDGETING THROUGH THE YEARS

Your three-year-old would probably not understand the difference between needs and wants, while getting your sixteen-year-old to start saving for college isn't giving him enough time. Your child will have different needs and priorities as he grows up. There is no fixed formula that works throughout. Here's what to focus on with your children over various age ranges.

Between four and seven years old

- Use the Save, Share and Spend jars to budget how to allocate their allowance (see Chapter 2). A good rule of thumb is to put at least 10 percent each towards Saving and Sharing. Older kids can be more flexible in their allocation.

Between eight and twelve years old

- Teach your children to tell wants apart from needs. It might get naggy but it's necessary. Do they need to have a banana split when you just baked yummy cookies at home? Should he buy another water gun when he needs money for his school recess time?

- Help them to analyse buying decisions by showing them how sales work. Explain that the video game he wants to buy can be purchased at a lower price if he does some simple research— online or during sales. Such a habit will allow them to make the most of their spending power as they grow.

- Let them have their own savings account (see Chapter 4) to encourage long-term savings to meet more advanced goals like saving for college or a school trip overseas they would like to go on the next year.

Between thirteen and eighteen years old

- Provide less handholding when your child is older. When kids become teenagers, they want to start making their own decisions. Learn to step back and let them be responsible for their own choices. It is better they make mistakes now, when the consequences are smaller, than make huge mistakes later.

SUMMARY

Budgeting helps your child to gain control over his money—your child learns to control his money rather than letting money control him. A budget is a way of being intentional about the way he spends and saves his money.

No matter how you slice it, there's a spending, savings and a sharing component to budgeting. No matter how young your child, budgeting can be mastered as soon as he is getting an allowance.

To balance a budget successfully, your child needs to understand the difference between needs and wants, and that sometimes tough decisions have to be made because of opportunity cost.

Quiz

1. **Your ten-year-old Linda says budgets are useless because they never balance—income is always more than expenses or the other way around. You:**
   a. Insist that her budgets continue to be made because like broccoli, it's good for her.
   b. Make adjustments by taking back some allowance or adding to it so that the budget balances.
   c. Stop for a few months and review in the future. Perhaps Tess is too young to manage a budget.
   d. Explain that budgets don't need to balance all the time. They are a plan to regularly review expenses and income.

(a) 3 (b) 1 (c) 1 (d) 3

We know that for adults, budgets seldom balance, if at all. But the whole exercise of working out a budget is absolutely essential in everyday family and business situations. For a business, making a budget means to plan ahead the essential tasks the company must undertake in order to attain business goals. The grand plan for a child is no different. For Tess, she would be learning to set aside money for important priorities (saving and sharing) and spending what's available on essential goods and services. Tess is old enough to manage a budget if she is already receiving an allowance. If she is in a new environment such as a new school or a new grade, you might consider stopping for a while or making adjustments to her allowance until her spending needs become clearer.

2. **Bessie wants the latest iPhone when her current phone works just fine. You:**

   a. Ask her to include saving for the iPhone as an item on her budget.

   b. Offer to pay half the upgrade price and she saves for the other half.

   c. Tell her she will have to wait till her birthday when she gets one as a gift.

   d. Buy the latest iPhone since all her classmates have upgraded their phones.

(a) 3 (b) 2 (c) 2 (d) 1

Wanting the latest iPhone presents a good opportunity to emphasise the importance of budgeting. By showing her how her savings can be channelled into a purchase in a few months, Bessie will be learning that she has to give up certain things in order to get what she really wants. Opportunity cost is the greatest teacher in helping us decide what truly is important in our lives. For Bessie, having less to buy chocolate and snacks helps her to focus on what's important to her. Of course she shouldn't be forgoing essential expenses like nutritious food and drinks.

3. **Johnny is arguing with you at the store that he wants you to buy his favourite ice cream or he would get ill. You:**
   a. Tell him that without ice cream he would do just fine.
   b. Make him pay for it himself as he's saved up some money.
   c. Buy the ice cream anyway but make sure he gets it in moderate amounts.
   d. Have him promise to keep his room clean for a week before he gets some.

(a) 2 (b) 1 (c) 3 (d) 0

Depriving a child of ice cream is like telling his father he cannot watch his favourite soccer team play on TV. Both are not needs in the sense that Johnny or his father would develop a bad illness if he is deprived of it. But it would make them pretty mad and miserable. Buying the ice cream for Johnny and letting him have some in moderation is a good way to teach discipline. Making him use his savings is not a good idea because those savings were meant to be used to purchase something else. This would make it too easy for him to go off budget and take away the importance of staying within budget.

CHAPTER 4
SAVING

Allowance + Other Income =
SAVING + Spending + Sharing

TREAT SAVING LIKE IT'S HAVING DESSERT

If spending is ice cream and saving is broccoli, which would your kids choose?

Thankfully since you have come to this chapter after learning how to deal with allowances and budgeting, saving should be a cinch. That means that your kid would have already decided on an amount each to save, spend and share.

Still, your child is sure to ask, "Why should I save money when spending is so much more fun?" How do we make saving a desirable habit for them?

START WITH SETTING SHORT-TERM SAVING GOALS

We suggest that you help your kids set short-term goals as the reason for saving so that they can enjoy what they saved up for after a period of two to three months. You can do this in three simple steps:

AT THE START	NEXT TWO MONTHS	AT THE END
Define the saving goal	Save before spending	Spend the savings

STEP 1—DEFINE SAVING GOAL

We must always save for a reason. Help your child to set a goal, one he can accomplish in a manageable amount of time. It could be a jersey from his favourite sports team or something sought-after that can be purchased in one to two months time. Having kids save up for their own toy or sneakers (instead of buying it for them) is a great way to teach them that putting aside small amounts of money today can pay off in big rewards later.

To help your child set manageable goals, you should discuss what he wants to buy, find out the price, and figure out how much he'll have to save every week to buy it by a certain date.

STEP 2—SAVE BEFORE SPENDING

Your child should always fill the savings jar first before spending. It's a simple way to spend on himself in the future. Here are some suggestions to encourage your child to save first before spending:

Stick a picture on the savings jar

Cut out a picture of the desired item and tape it onto the savings jar. As your child puts more money in the jar, she literally sees the money grow towards her goal. An older child could keep track of savings in a ledger and redo the calculations each week.

Offer rewards for saving money

Consider rewarding your child for saving his money. It need not be monetary. Try giving stickers, an extra hour for playing video games or whatever motivates your child.

But it can also be monetary. Try matching your child's savings; it doesn't have to be dollar for dollar. Perhaps a bonus of $0.20 for every dollar saved. This can be a great way to encourage your child to save extra.

Have your own savings jar

Encourage your child to save by letting him see that you save money too. Keep your own savings jar and put money into it while your child is watching. Explain what you are saving for and your child will learn that saving is normal. Most young children want to be like their parents, and they will want to mimic you to save.

Be frugal to save more

Show your frugal side by explaining how you are using coupons at the grocery store or looking for sales in the newspapers and showing them the savings. When saving money becomes an important priority in the family, it will have a trickle-down effect on even the youngest kids.

STEP 3—SPEND THE SAVINGS

Time's up. Money's saved. Time to spend. Yippee!

As a parent or caregiver, it's time to take your hands off. Your kids saved hard the past few months. Now they want to go to the store to get the toy they have been saving for. It is an achievement for kids to set a goal and work towards it. Let them enjoy and be rewarded for that success.

Long-term savings

When your kids become older, like from their early- to mid-teens, you will want to teach them about long-term savings. In fact, once kids reach twelve years of age, you should consider insisting that a percentage of their allowance goes into a long-term savings account that can be invested when they are older.

I got every one of these toys from my own savings!

Start with a piggy bank

You can have your child create a fourth jar labelled 'Long-term Savings' or buy a nice piggy bank for him to save long-term money in his room. We prefer a piggy bank so that it can be differentiated from a savings jar.

One of the greatest joys of saving we remember as kids was when we turned our coins into larger and larger notes. When your child's savings reach $45 or more, remove all the coins and give your child a $50 note.

Piggy banks didn't start off as piggies

The use of piggy banks dates back to the fifteenth century when savings jars were crafted from 'pygg', which is a type of clay. Over the years, the 'piggy bank' evolved.

You can find many fun piggy banks today that are not piggies at all. Just search on Amazon or eBay and you will come across:

- Piggy banks in the shape of Mickey Mouse, Hello Kitty and Darth Vader.
- Shine Itazura Stealing Coin Bank. While the lid is closed, place a coin on top of a white plate. The lid opens to reveal a cute little panda who peeks out and then snatches the coin with its paw.
- Dreams Money-saving BanClock. The Banclock will sound an alarm every morning and will not shut up unless you feed it a coin.

OPENING A SAVINGS ACCOUNT AT THE BANK

Your child's piggy bank is filled to the top! Now it's time to find a savings account for him to deposit his coins and notes and watch the money grow even more. Banks offer many types of savings accounts for kids to encourage them to be savers from as young as seven years old.

Having a savings account at a bank will show your child two important things:

- Where money is kept and deposited.
- What interest is and how money grows as a result.

When opening a savings account, look out for:

- *Fees and Requirements.* Most children accounts do not charge fees and have low minimum balance requirements. Some even allow coins to be deposited up till a certain age.
- *Passbooks.* Some savings accounts provide passbooks so your child can keep track of his savings account balance. This is an essential tracking tool.
- *Interest Rates.* The savings accounts should earn an interest even if it is very low. It will be much easier to explain the power of compounding if the account is earning interest.

EXPLAIN THE CONCEPT OF INTEREST RATES

When you deposit money into the bank, it lends your money out as loans to borrowers and charges them interest. Interest is like a rental payment that borrowers pay for the use of the bank's money. In the same way, for the use of your money, the bank pays you interest. Interest is a percentage of the amount you have on deposit. For example, if you deposit $10,000 in the bank and it pays you 2 percent interest per year, then after one year, the bank will pay you $200 in interest ($10,000 × 2%). Assuming you leave the money in the bank, the total amount would now be $10,200. If you were to continue to leave the entire amount in the bank at the same rate of interest, then after another year, your balance would rise to $10,404 ($10,200 × 1.02). This is the effect of compounding, where the interest you earn in year one is used to earn even more interest in the second year.

Adam says

My wife and I teach our children that a dollar bill is like a money seed. If you spend the seed, it is gone forever. However, if you plant the seed by saving and investing that dollar, it would grow into a money tree that will grow hundreds more dollar bills. The idea that money can grow into more money excites them and we show them how the money they saved from their allowance and from their red packet collection during Chinese New Year has grown in the form of interest and dividends.

From the time they were little, we would put their savings into stocks and Real Estate Investment Trusts (REITs). We would then show them the quarterly statements and they see how their money grows— like magic. They get so fascinated that when we ask them if they would like to draw the money out to spend, they shake their heads and say, "No! Let it grow ... don't kill the money seed." This lays a great foundation for them to be future savers and investors.

Quiz

1. **Ten-year-old Denise says, "I have $80 in my savings jar. I am going to buy a box of Godiva chocolates as I had planned." You:**
   a. Let Denise buy the chocolates since she saved for them.
   b. Pay for the chocolates so that she can maintain her piggy bank balance.
   c. Refuse to let her withdraw from her piggy bank as the savings should be for college.
   d. Tell her that she cannot spend $80 on a box of chocolates when she can get a box of good chocolates for $10.

   (a) 3 (b) 0 (c) 0 (d) 2
   If it was Denise's plan to save for the Godiva chocolates and you had agreed to that plan, then nothing should stop her from buying the chocolates. If the plan was for chocolates in general, then you will want to add that $80 for a box of chocolate is very costly and that a $10 box would do. The issue then is that the savings goal was not stated clearly enough. Like other goals, savings goals must be SMART (specific, measurable, attainable, realistic and timely).

2. **Your ten-year-old asks, "Why don't you just press some money out of the ATM?" You:**
   a. Say that money doesn't grow on trees.
   b. Say that the ATM machine is out of money.
   c. Explain that the ATM is like a piggy bank and money is limited.
   d. Explain that you cannot be pressing for money whenever you feel like it.

(a) 1 (b) 0 (c) 3 (d) 1

The worst thing to say is to make something up that isn't true. Tell your child that the ATM is like an electronic piggy bank into which your money goes when you receive income from your job. And like your child, you have to manage your limited funds for saving, spending and sharing—just like he does.

3. **Kelly has not put money into her savings jar for the past two weeks. You:**
   a. Insist that she starts putting in money again.
   b. Give her extra money to put into the savings jar.
   c. Review her budget to see if she needs more money.
   d. Offer her a savings match of $0.20 for every dollar she puts in.

(a) 2 (b) 0 (c) 3 (d) 2

This is a good time to review her money needs. Unless she has been pinching some money to buy unplanned items, her allowance may need to be increased. If her spending needs have not changed, then you should insist on Kelly continuing to feed the savings jar. Offering a savings match is always useful but it should only be for the purpose of the current savings goal. It should not be a permanent feature.

4. **Nick has $2,000 in his college savings account in the bank. He wants to use half of that for a new PlayStation. You:**
   a. Say his current PlayStation works just fine.
   b. Refuse to let him because the savings are for college.
   c. Help him establish a short-term savings goal to buy the PlayStation.
   d. Buy him a new PlayStation since he has done a good job saving for college.

(a) 1 (b) 3 (c) 3 (d) 0
The objective of the college savings account is plainly for college expenses in the future. It should not be used for any other purpose unless there is an emergency. Establish a new short-term goal to save enough for the PlayStation. As the machine costs a few hundred dollars, you may have to stretch the duration of the savings schedule, offer a savings match or buy it for his birthday if it's coming up in a few months' time.

SUMMARY

Teach your kids that saving is a virtue but it has fun outcomes too. Let them spend the cash after they have saved it, even if it cleans them out. For kids, letting them spend is just reward for their saving.

Sure, you could just give them hard cash if you can afford it, but having saved for something themselves, they will have learnt patience, discipline and hopefully money smarts.

Remember to praise your child when they follow through with saving. It means that your child was able to set a spending goal, save for it and then enjoy the fruits of his labours.

CHAPTER 5
SPENDING

Jenny gets her weekly allowance

Chocolate. Pizza. Video games.

School books. Lunch. Bus.

Allowance + Other Income =
Saving + **SPENDING** + Sharing

THE MOST IMPORTANT MONEY CONCEPT

What is the most important money concept to teach children? Many of us may say 'saving money'. While we wouldn't be wrong, we would only be half right. That's because most of our money is allocated to spending. Teaching children how to spend wisely is equally, if not more, important.

Spend according to budget

At this stage, you have already sat down with your child to plan what and how much he needs to spend. There is no further need to do anything else at this stage, except to monitor and help your child to spend wisely and according to plan.

Adam says

The allowance that we give to our children are strictly only for essential needs like food, stationery and transport. As for 'wants' like toys, games and special treats, they have to earn the money by doing chores and accumulating points from good behaviour.

In order to be effective, we have to enforce the expectations and rules we have set for our children and not cave in when they break the rules. There was once we discovered that our daughter had spent her daily food allowance on candy and playing cards. She was eating bread and drinking water instead of using the money on a proper meal.

When we found out, we had to enforce the consequences of her poor spending decision. She was denied a food allowance for the next three days and was given bread and water instead for her packed lunch. She learnt the important lesson of not wasting her money on non-essential items.

Let them make mistakes early

Learning to spend wisely involves trial and error and it may even take a while (many adults still haven't mastered this skill). If you give your child an allowance and insist on approving all purchases, this would stifle his decision-making and the money lesson could be lost or watered down.

Suppose your daughter spends her entire weekly allowance on Pokemon cards. Three days later, she sees a jigsaw puzzle she really wants. What would you do? Don't give in to her pleas for more money. In fact, you should be delighted because this is precisely the message you are trying to get across—that when it comes to dealing with money, she needs to plan ahead and follow the budget. Luckily, she will learn this lesson when the consequences are less serious. Not having a jigsaw puzzle at age ten is a lot more manageable than not being able to pay a $5,000 credit card bill at age twenty-five.

Monitoring how the allowance is spent

The lesson for parents is that once you hand over the money, you have to leave your hands off and stay aside. The money is no longer yours and your child decides how it should be spent. After all, you want your child to think for himself when it comes to money.

You may nevertheless want to place some expectations on how your child spends it. But how much influence should you apply? Can you insist that a certain percentage of the allowance go towards lunch? Can you dictate that your child pays for all her movie tickets? There are no hard-and-fast rules.

On one hand, you can say nothing and let your child make all his own decisions. On the other hand, you can set conditions on how the allowance should be allocated among different categories of planned expenditure. Somewhere in the middle is where you'll probably want to fall. Of course, it goes without saying that your child should know that the allowance will stop immediately if it is used for cigarettes, alcohol or illegal activities.

KEEP A LOG TO MONITOR SPENDING

Have your child keep a daily log on his spending. Give him a notebook to carry with him all the time. Have him start a new page for each new day and write the date at the top. Then compare with the budget plan at the end of each week.

Date:

Purchased Item	Amount	Planned or Unplanned

Overspending (making unplanned purchases)

If your kid is overbuying, mostly on unplanned purchases, you should step in to help adjust her spending. Say she is overbuying Rainbow Loom Rubber Band sets. You might want to set the rule that once she owns three sets, she has to give away or swap an old set for every new set she buys. Or if she is overbuying books, you could restrict the number of books she owns to no more than what can be stored on her bookshelf.

Making your kids budget shoppers

Instead of letting your kid pay $100 from her savings for an expensive pair of jeans, show her how to pick up a designer pair on sale or from a factory outlet sale for $60 and save $40 for other clothing items.

Encourage your child to trade things like books and electronic games with his friends, and to alter items like clothes that do not fit instead of getting new ones.

Or if they are not old enough to trade, you can help do it for them by hosting a toy swap. If you have preschoolers, chances are that you probably have a whole pile of toys at home that your kids don't even look at anymore.

Hosting a toy swap

A toy swap is a great way to exchange unused or little-used toys for new ones that your little one might enjoy at little to no cost. Everyone wins. Here's how.

1. *Decide on a guest list.* Invite about ten friends with children who are close in age to yours. We recommend leaving the kids at home to avoid any whining or tantrums over the toys.

2. *Set rules.* Each friend brings at least five toys. The toys must be in decent condition. That means puzzles that aren't missing pieces. Plastic toys should be wiped clean. Pick toys that other kids might genuinely enjoy—even if your kids don't even notice them anymore. Provide one ticket for every toy that each parent brings; each ticket allows the parents to choose one toy from the pool. If the values of the toys are vastly different, give a ticket for every dollar in value of the toy. A $5 toy would get five tickets to go towards redeeming someone else's toy.

3. *Display.* When the parents arrive, set up their toys in a large enough area for easy and comfortable browsing. You may want to group the water guns together, boy toys on one table, girl toys in the corner, baby toys somewhere else.

4. *Swap.* Have each guest pick a number so they select their toys in an orderly manner. Or don't take turns and let everyone take what they want. Every now and then, there may be a great parent-fight over the hottest items, but this should rarely happen.

5. *Donate.* Anything that's left over at the end of the swap can be donated to your local shelter or favourite non-profit organisation.

A few other ideas for swap parties are books and clothings.

COOLING-OFF PERIODS FOR UNPLANNED EXPENDITURE

Cooling-off periods work for kids, just as they do for adults. They help to keep the child from making rash purchases. Here's how: Say you are at Forever 21 with your kid and she sees this $39 blouse that she's just got to have. Insist on a three-day cooling-off period before she is able to buy the blouse. After three days, there is a good chance that she will find something else that she would rather spend her money on. If she still wants the item, then you know it's an item she needs or really likes and has spent time thinking about it.

DON'T BAIL THEM OUT

We can't say this enough. None of your money lessons will have any staying power if you keep handing your kids more money when they run out and fail to keep to their budgeted plan. They need to learn that the choices they make have consequences in their lives. The earlier they learn that lesson, the better off they will be.

Quiz

1. **You just gave Matthew his allowance for the week. After putting away portions for saving and for sharing, he wants to spend the remaining amount on a video game. You:**
   a. Let him buy the video game.
   b. Offer to buy the game for his birthday.
   c. Offer to pay a portion so he does not exhaust his allowance.
   d. Refuse to let him buy the game as it is an 'off-limit' item.

(a) 0 (b) 2 (c) 1 (d) 3
Not only is the game an off-limit item, it would exhaust his allowance. How would he last the week without money for essential items like food and transport? The price of the video game is likely to be more than a week's allowance. Encourage him to set up a short-term savings goal to purchase the game.

2. **Sandra wants a $50 Lego Superheroes set for her birthday. You:**
   a.   Check eBay for a lightly used set.
   b.   Take money out of her savings jar to buy it.
   c.   Buy it at the toy store since it is her birthday.
   d.   Tell Grandma that she can buy that for Sandra.

(a) 3 (b) 0 (c) 3 (d) 3
Birthdays are special days on which kids should be treated to their favourite foods and showered with gifts—$50 for a toy is not an unreasonable amount.

3. **Freddie spent almost his entire weekly allowance on the first day and he doesn't have enough money for lunch for the rest of the week. You:**
   a.   Refuse to give him any more. Do not bail him out.
   b.   Top up and make sure he has enough for lunch and essentials, and no more.
   c.   Give him next week's allowance and have him manage his spending the next two weeks.
   d.   Explain the difference between needs and wants, and top up his weekly allowance.

(a) 2 (b) 3 (c) 3 (d) 0
Freddie wrecked his budget plan and he must learn a lesson. While we should not bail him out, we still need to make sure he has enough for essentials. If he has enough allowance left for essentials then do not bail him out. Let him skip his sweets, movies and outings for a week. Chances are that he will be more careful the following week.

4. **Your twelve-year-old has a kind heart. He treats three of his friends to lunch and movies, and runs out of allowance. You:**
   a. Do not bail him out. He made unplanned expenses.
   b. Top up his allowance. Kind acts should always be rewarded.
   c. Caution him about letting his friends take advantage of his kindness.
   d. Tell him that his kindness has led him to overspend.

(a) 3 (b) 1 (c) 2 (d) 3

Oversharing is no different from overspending. In the end, someone has to pay. If your child displays frequent acts of over-kindness he needs to understand that the money has to come out of his pocket and he needs to exercise restraint. The other important lesson, a cynical but practical one, is that there are those who would exploit a person's kindness for their own selfish benefit. Your child will have to learn one day that there are such things as cheats and scams especially in the adult world.

SUMMARY

Part of making good spending choices is being aware of the difference between needs and wants. We covered this key concept in Chapter 3 on budgeting and it is a lesson worth repeating. Needs are things such as nutritious food and transport. After his needs are paid for, your child might have some money left over for wants. Since we usually have more wants than we can afford, kids have to make choices and decide what they really want the most. Kids can learn at an early age that money is limited and they have to make spending choices.

Children make choices every day—what to wear, what snack to have at recess, which video game to play. Each day is filled with options, and even very young children are capable of making simple decisions. If children are encouraged to make choices, then making important decisions as they get older will be easier because they will have the experience and confidence.

CHAPTER 6
SHARING AND GIVING

Allowance + Other Income = Saving
+ Spending + **SHARING**

SHARING IS THE KEY TO A HAPPY LIFE

Your child knows by now how much from his allowance he needs to share. (We use the words sharing and giving synonymously.) But he is still asking you, why share when he hardly has enough money for himself?

Giving is not a lesson that can be taught today and applied right away tomorrow. It is a lesson that takes time to sink in over the years but the benefits of regular giving last a lifetime.

Sharing is part of authentic happiness

In his leading research on happiness, psychologist Martin Seligman maintains that it takes three types of lives integrated together to bring us Authentic Happiness—the Pleasant Life, the Good Life and the Meaningful Life.[6]

- *The Pleasant Life* is about having a lot of positive feelings about the present, past and the future. Having a delicious banana split or a beach holiday during Christmas brings about a positive feeling. This type of life does not, by itself, lead to authentic happiness, but it does put the icing on the cake of a happy life.

- *The Good Life* is about experiencing an engaged life by identifying your highest strengths and talents, and finding opportunities to use those strengths. If you are good at counting or communicating, you can have an engaged life if you use those strengths in work, love, play, friendship and parenting.

- *The Meaningful Life* involves sharing your highest strengths and talents to serve something that is bigger than yourself. This can be to give your time and efforts to your community, an orphanage or a religious institution.

---

6   For more information, visit www.authentichappiness.sas.upenn.edu

Giving should be for a reason

At this stage, your focus is to help your child understand why it is important to share and to cultivate a giving heart. Religious giving is one of the best ways to get your child started in giving—whether your family is Muslim, Christian, Hindu or of some other faith. For example, tithing (giving one-tenth of one's income to a religious organisation or charity) is part of the Christian faith. So if your child gets $10 a week as an allowance, he could be giving about $1 through tithing.

"I don't have much money to give!"

Your child may be getting an allowance of $5 a week and the $0.50 he is adding to his sharing jar doesn't seem like much. But remind your child that it all adds up in the end:

- *Even a small amount is worth giving.* Skipping a Starbucks Frappuccino once a month could give him $5 or more for giving.
- *She can save her spare change at any time.* Her sharing jar is where she can drop her spare change into.
- *Set up a family sharing jar in the kitchen.* Ask your family members to drop in any change they have at any time.

Adam says

We believe that it is very important for our children to develop the habit of being generous and giving to the less fortunate. When they collect their red packet money every Lunar New Year, we will ask them to set aside a percentage to be given to charity (our temple, elderly homes, children's home, etc). We will also regularly ask our children to donate some of their toys to underprivileged children. They were a bit reluctant to do so initially, "Why should I give my toys away to other people?" they would grumble. However, when we let them present their toys or money to underprivileged children and they receive all the praise, they start to associate a lot of love and good feelings with giving. This builds a good foundation for their future.

GIVING IS NOT JUST ABOUT MONEY

As your children grow up, they begin to understand that others have less than they do. They can learn to share with people in many ways. For example:

- They can give a part of their money.
- They can help people by giving their time and energy.
- They can share or give away clothes and toys they no longer use, by passing them on to others who have a use for them.

Some giving ideas include:

- *Donating clothes.* Periodically have your child go through his cupboard for clothes and toys he hasn't used in a while, which can be given to the Salvation Army for distribution to the needy. Allow him to select which clothes or toys he wishes to donate. Take your child with you when you drop the items off at the collection point.

- *Helping neighbours.* Discuss with your child on an activity she can regularly perform, such as baking cookies or cleaning windows. Then find persons such as an elderly neighbour or a welfare organisation that will accept your child's contributions.
- *Throwing a charitable birthday party.* Set up birthday parties as a time for giving to others. Ask guests to bring a gift of a book or teddy bear to be donated to a local charity. Have your child decide whether to give to a senior citizen's home, a home for the disabled or some other organisation.
- *Taking a volunteer vacation.* Your child could teach English to students in to build a home for a homeless family. Volunteer vacations can bring enriching experiences and friendships that help forge the spirit of giving.[7]

---

7   Do be careful about sending your kids around the world. Many organisations have sprung up in recent years that may be more profit-driven than mission-driven. Sometimes volunteerism can harm the community by taking jobs away from local workers and generate emotional attachment issues with children. At other times volunteers are not trained sufficiently and they may not know what's safe or unsafe. See Tristin Hopper, " 'Voluntourism': Mixing vacations with charity work can harm as much as it helps," *National Post*, 19 April 2013, www.news.nationalpost.com.

Keon says

I taught English every Saturday for four years at a senior citizens home. I taught them to sing English songs like "Twinkle Twinkle Little Star" and "Silent Night" and brought them to other homes to perform on stage. Many of my students were in their seventies and eighties. They were so eager to learn that they brought tape recorders to class—they wanted so much to be able to communicate with their grandchildren. Sarah was studying in the US and whenever she was back in Singapore, she would join me to teach or just be around to help tidy up. Those few experiences we had together made an impression on her. Today, she volunteers her time regularly in Arizona to various charities like the March of Dimes (premature babies), Toys for Tots and animal shelters.

CULTIVATE A GIVING HEART

Have you come across a person who may be giving away loads of money at a time each month but without a giving heart? We can force our children to give, but without a giving heart and the genuine desire to help other people, the 'giving' becomes taking away something that your child may be unwilling to let go of, such as a toy or money (even if someone else needs it more). We want our children to give joyfully.

To understand what we mean, let's look at what Jack and his two children Penny and Lucus do every Christmas:

Once a year on Christmas day, Jack brings his children to the children's home to distribute sandwiches, give away their old clothes and toys, and sing Christmas carols with the children. He takes many photos of the trip to remind his children of how fortunate they are in comparison. His donations entitles him to a deduction on his income taxes. Jack feels this annual trip gives him and his children a sense of giving back, and he feels fulfilled by this.

What do you see that is good or can be better, about what Jack is teaching his children about giving? Here are some of our insights.

Giving should be regular

Make giving the rule rather than the exception. Giving should not be reserved only for emergencies or special occasions. You will be helping your children appreciate that reaching out to others in need is a way of life, rather than a moment in time when a disaster occurs or when Santa is coming to town.

Remember, while you are giving to others, you are giving your children important messages about your beliefs concerning the spirit of giving. If they see you giving regularly and hear you talk about it often, they will want to do it too. Be intentional about the family giving. Make time for it. Make it a priority.

Jack may want to consider a family activity that takes place on a more regular basis. It could be as simple as visiting the children's home once every month.

Giving should be based on what your child is comfortable doing

Children should see their money actually going to charity to appreciate that their giving is benefiting others. They should also be comfortable sharing their talents in an activity they enjoy and can relate to.

Jackson knew that both Penny and Lucus like making sandwiches and singing. So it wasn't difficult for him to take them to visit the home. Now if he were to visit the home once a month, the children may need to take on some regular chores that they are not crazy about like mopping and cleaning. Your family has to accept that in giving, we sometimes have to go beyond our comfort zones to help others.

We could fall into despair anytime. If you saw yourself
on the street wouldn't you give to yourself?

Giving should be sincere

Children should give when they really wish to give. You should
never pressure them to give or when it seems fashionable to do so
(such as donating to an earthquake disaster because several media
stars are doing so).

Never give as an opportunity for self-promotion (such as
wanting to be seen to be generous). Your child should find out
what it is that is needed rather than just give away what would
be disposed of anyway. Do not treat the charity collection centre
like a trash can. For Penny and Lucus, the toys and clothes they
give away should be good items that they themselves would want
if they didn't have them in the first place. They should not be
armless dolls or playing cards with the King of Hearts missing.

Always involve your child in deciding who to give to

Let your child decide what's important to her and find the charities
that address her giving aspirations. Discuss your child's concerns
about the world. Does he want to help cure a particular disease?

Support the arts? Support a religious organisation? This type of discussion will help your child identify the areas that he'd like to help. Then find the charity that's trying to fix the problems your child is concerned about. Maybe a well-known charity comes to mind.

For Penny and Lucus, their grandfather died of heart disease a year ago and they want to donate money to the Heart Foundation. At the same time, they enjoy meeting other children.

Quiz

1. **Matthew sees a premium $40 baseball cap he wants to buy and he wants to take $20 from his sharing money. He would rather spend on himself than on other people. You:**
    a. Ask him to save for it.
    b. Refuse to allow him to buy it.
    c. Review and reinforce the reasons for sharing.
    d. Buy it and deduct $20 from next week's allowance.

(a) 2 (b) 2 (c) 3 (d) 1

It's clear that unplanned items should never factor into spending decisions. This would ruin the budget and the allowance plan. Unplanned items should be saved for and there should be no exception. If there is a reason that the purchase should be made right away, such as it's the last piece remaining, then you may consider making an exception. But make sure he accounts for the $20 by deducting it from his allowance or through some other means. The greater lesson is to help Matthew understand the reasons for sharing which he does not yet appreciate. This lesson may take years to sink in but the benefits of happiness and contentment are well worth the effort.

2. **Ten-year-old Susan and you have been visiting the senior citizens' home every first Sunday of the month. The place needs a good mopping each time. Mopping is tiring for her and she would rather help out in the kitchen. You:**

   a. Work with her together in the kitchen.
   b. Let her help out in the kitchen instead.
   c. Ask her to share the mopping with other volunteers.
   d. Insist she mops the floor because volunteering isn't supposed to be fun.

(a) 1 (b) 2 (c) 3 (d) 2

A balance needs to be struck between what must be done and what your child is comfortable doing. If volunteering is all fun and laughter then we would be awash with volunteers everywhere. In the end, floors have to be mopped and windows wiped. For your children's efforts in sharing their time and efforts to be sustainable, a large part of what they give should be on activities and causes they enjoy and believe in. For Susan, a good balance is to have her mop once every other month or perhaps for a short period of time on each visit.

3. **Your son John refuses to share his toys with his friend Jack who has come over to visit. You:**
   a. Punish John for not sharing.
   b. Put some of his favourite toys away.
   c. Promise John an ice cream if he shares his toys.
   d. Force John to share because sharing is an obligation of every family member.

(a) 1 (b) 3 (c) 1 (d) 1

Children become attached to things just as you are to your favourite coffee mug. When your child refuses to share his favourite toy truck, he isn't really being selfish—he's just acting his age. To reduce some of the tantrums, try letting your child hide a few of his most favourite toys before his friends come over. Tell him these toys are ones he doesn't have to share, then put them away. Make sure there are plenty left that John doesn't mind sharing. You should not punish him for not sharing. Let him work this out with other children. When he doesn't share, his friends will let him know how unhappy they are, and he'll learn that it takes hard work and lots of give and take to be a good friend. Giving an ice cream may work but don't offer bribes too often. Otherwise he will expect to be rewarded each time for sharing anything.

4. **Your daughter Rose loves sharing so much that she runs out of allowance each week when she shares her spending money with her friends. You:**
   a. Tell her that she needs to spend and share within her budget.
   b. Find out if she is being forced or bullied into sharing her money.
   c. Let her continue and top up her allowance because sharing should always be encouraged.
   d. Give her daily instead of weekly allowances until she learns to regulate her spending and sharing.

(a) 2 (b) 3 (c) 1 (d) 3

If your child is always the grabber, she'll learn that other kids won't want to play with her. On the other hand, if she's always the victim, she needs to learn to say 'no.' Telling her she has to stay within her budget works only if you know why she's oversharing. There should be a limit to sharing especially when an amount was budgeted for in her allowance so topping up her allowance ruins the allowance plan. If she has problems adjusting because she cannot yet handle lump sum allowances, then break the allowance into smaller amounts and give it to her on a daily basis.

5. **Your job pays modestly and you live on a tight budget. The amount of allowance you give your son Zack isn't enough to allow him to set much aside for sharing. You:**
   a. Tell Zack to reduce his spending and/or saving in order to share.
   b. Insist that he sets aside an amount for sharing even if it's very little.
   c. Tell him he doesn't need to set anything for sharing until a later time.
   d. Ask him to share by doing errands for free for your elderly neighbours.

(a) 3 (b) 3 (c) 1 (d) 3

There are many ways to share. Sharing isn't only about money. It can be using your time and energy to help a neighbour. Sharing can take place every day and not only when you have enough money. A few cents a day adds up to a few dollars a month.

SUMMARY

There is much sadness in the world. More than 6 million children die each year from preventable diseases, and over 1 billion people lack access to clean drinking water.[8] Fortunately there are unlimited ways to make a positive difference by giving. Your child will make new friends, achieve a sense of pride and live happier lives through giving.

Keep in mind that giving should begin at home. Charles Dickens said, "Charity begins at home, and justice begins next door." If we really want to make the world a better place, start by being polite to your neighbours and always greeting your family with a smile. There are probably many examples of people who give away thousands of dollars to charity but leave little heart or dollars for their own families.

---

8   For more information, see www.givingwhatwecan.org

CHAPTER 7
OTHER INCOME

Allowance + **OTHER INCOME** =
Saving + Spending + Sharing

Besides receiving allowance, kids have all sorts of opportunities to obtain other income, such as from birthday gifts and unplanned Grandparent dollars. While these opportunities provide a good other source of income, they do not take place on a regular basis. What parents can do is to teach their kids how to earn extra regular money through their own efforts and by investing.

EARNING MONEY FROM THEIR OWN EFFORTS

Parents should encourage kids to work even if they can provide for them. An old saying goes, "You really don't understand the true value of money until you have earned it yourself." By encouraging your kids to work, you can effectively teach your children the value of money and help them to understand that money does not grow on trees.

When can kids begin to earn?

At some point your child may feel that his allowance isn't enough for his spending and saving, and he would like to earn some additional money. That's when he can begin.

Earning from a regular or holiday job is a great way to teach your kids about responsibility, how to present themselves to others, and handling money.

You will need to find out the child labour laws in the country that you live, and whatever rules there are that regulate the employment of minors. For example:

- In Singapore, children of twelve years and above may be employed to do light work in a non-industrial undertaking. McDonald's for instance can hire your child if he is fourteen years old. Children below the age of fourteen years are not allowed to work in an industrial undertaking unless it is a family business where only family members are employed. An industrial undertaking includes factories, shipyards and transport operators.[9]

- In Hong Kong, children aged twelve and younger may not work at all except in the entertainment field.

Preparation for work

Prepare your child for work so that he can succeed and his confidence is positively boosted. Help your child to make a list of tasks and skills that are appropriate for his age. Use the following questionnaire to guide your child.

Work Questionnaire (to be filled in by your child)

1. What will I do?
2. What do I need to know to do the job?
3. When will I conduct my business?
4. What will be the name of my business?
5. Is there a need for my product or service?
6. Who will be my customers?
7. Who else is doing this business?
8. How much are they charging?
9. How much will I charge?
10. How much time will each job take?

---

9   For more information, see www.lawsociety.org.sg/forPublic/YoutheLaw/Employment.aspx

11. How much money do I want to make?
12. What kind of equipment do I need?
13. How much money do I need to start my business?
14. What kind of help do I need from my parents?
15. Do I need other people's help?
16. How will I advertise my services?

If your child goes door-to-door in search of work, make sure that he understands that presentation and politeness count. He should visit people you know such as neighbours and relatives. Print business cards with a photograph of your child. His prospects would be impressed.

Get a name card or CV printed

Let me introduce myself...

I'm Henry Gopal, twelve years old and I am a tutor in English and mathematics. For the past two years, I have been tutoring my younger sister and kids in Primary 1 to 4 (ages six to ten). I am a responsible, conscientious tutor who loves children.

You can reach me at +65 1234 5678. The best time to call is between 4:00pm and 7:30pm. I charge $10 an hour and many of my students have become top scorers.

If you would like to speak to my references, please contact me for their names and contact details.

As you can see, your child should approach his job search as well prepared as would an adult. Let's take tutoring as the job your child has selected. Learn what makes a good tutor and whether your child is suitable. For example, a good tutor:

- Assists others in learning and not doing the work for another student.
- Knows good tutoring techniques such as making sure the student knows what is expected, giving good feedback to the student and keeping records of the tutoring session.
- Listens closely to the student and understands the assignment before helping the student.

The key is to match your child's skills, hobbies and talents with money-making opportunities. Here are ideas to earn money at home, in the neighbourhood and everywhere else.

Earning money at home

Do extra chores at home. Dusting furniture, vacuuming, sweeping floors and polishing shoes are all good ideas. Allow your kids to negotiate the best deal they can although between $5 and $10 an

hour sounds to us like a fair rate. While there is no minimum wage in Singapore, a basic wage of S$1,000 was set for cleaners in 2014. Using this as a convenient benchmark, a fair rate could be S$250 per week, S$50 per day or about S$6.25 an hour. Remember that these are extra chores on top of what they should normally do to help support a clean household.

Keon says

We have lots of old photos in our home. I had one of my Dad in the seventies giving Spookie, our first dog, a shower. Another showed my mother in her forties on roller skates, which was the first and last time I ever saw her skate. One school vacation when Sarah was ten, I got her to ask Grandpa to write on the back of each old photo what the photo was about. That was a wonderful time for the both of them.

Re-sell stuff online. Enter "sell used clothes" or "sell used books" and you will find many websites on which your children can sell their pre-loved and lightly-used items. And while there, you can also keep an eye out for 'hot' items at attractively reduced prices (even for yourself!).

Earning money in the neighbourhood

Join a neighbourhood garage sale. Your kids have plenty of toys sitting in the back of their wardrobe that haven't been played with for months or years. And they are mixed together with loads of clothes that they have grown out of. Find out about flea markets in your neighbourhood, reserve a space and enjoy a fun-filled family day together.

Run errands and do odd jobs for your neighbours. This is where making your presence known becomes important. If Mr and Mrs Suradi from the next block know that an enthusiastic and well-behaved youngster will happily wash their car, buy milk from the grocery store or wipe the book shelves, they might not go calling on family members for help. Visit the neighbours you know (avoid strangers!) with your kids to inform them that your kids are looking for odd jobs here and there. Most people have something they want to get done but keep putting aside. Ask them what your kids could help them with.

Earning money using technical skills

Teach someone how to use their computer and smart phone. Kids these days learn to use the computer from an early age and they use the latest word processing and spreadsheet applications in their school work. Tell your baby boomer friends and relatives that your kid is available to teach them how to create a Powerpoint presentation, upload music and movies to their smart phone or save digital photos to the cloud or Facebook.

Sell crafts or play music. If your kids are artistically inclined, put that to good use. We know of a children's book author who hired child artists to illustrate her storybooks. We know of a boy who plays three to five songs on a piano at weddings (including the Wedding March of course).

What kids learn by earning money from their own efforts

Even if you have the means, having your kids get a job to earn extra income is an excellent way of preparing him for the big wide world out there. He will learn how to present himself, value money even more through his own efforts and possibly discover what he would like to do when he is older. Most of all, he will learn that money is not easy to come by, but with effort anyone with skills and enthusiasm can earn it.

EARNING MONEY FROM INVESTING

Now that kids have money, besides saving it they can invest it. Investing means to buy something to keep that offers potential appreciation in value. For example, your child could buy a 1959 Superman comic book on eBay and then watch its price (hopefully) grow. For most people, buying stocks and bonds is the obvious way to invest. That's because stocks and bonds are commonly available through large securities exchanges like Singapore Exchange (SGX). Another reason is that the goods sold by many large companies are already popular with kids such as McDonald's, Mattel (makers of Barbie) and Walt Disney.

Explaining investing to your children

Investing means to put money to good use by purchasing something that is expected to increase in value or provide stable income over time. This is easy enough a definition for an adult but how do you explain something rather alien like a stock or bond to a ten-year-old?

The challenge for parents is in convincing their children that they should invest their money when spending it can be so much more fun. You can tell your child that by investing, he can have more income in the future than he can earn from his own efforts. Does investing bring good income over time? Let's use the example of Mikey Sport Shoes to help us out.

Everyone loves sports shoes for running and kicking soccer balls. How can investing in a company that makes sports shoes help increase income over time? This is how you can explain to your child that investing works.

Explaining why investing works

Suppose there is a company called Mikey Sports Shoes that makes sports shoes. A company refers to a group of people who come together to achieve a common business goal such as to sell hamburgers or to provide computer services.

If there are ten workers and each makes one pair of shoes a month, this company can make ten pairs of shoes a month. If the company doubles the number of employees to twenty, it can produce a total of twenty pairs of shoes. Because of higher employment, the company now produces twice what it produced before.

Next suppose that special technology is introduced that cuts down the amount of time needed to make a pair of shoes. Now each worker can make three pairs of shoes. Mikey Shoes' production has shot up to sixty pairs of shoes a month.

This is one of the most fundamental principles in investing. Higher employment and technology increases production. Since either or both of these factors are always increasing and improving, we can expect the value of companies to go up over the long term.

When companies need to raise money

When companies need to raise money to buy machinery or to hire more employees, they typically do so by issuing stocks and bonds. People who purchase stocks and bonds are in effect lending money to the company. Stocks and bonds are thus two of the most common instruments to invest in.

Owning a stock

When you buy a stock you become one of the owners or shareholders of the company. As a shareholder, you do not run the company. Rather it is run by employees and managers who are hired to run the show. When the company sells shoes and makes a profit, management decides whether to keep the profits to expand the business (by buying more materials to make more shoes), or to distribute the profits in the form of dividends (which is like a year-end bonus for employees).

As a shareholder, you are exposed to investment risk. The reason is that the company's earnings are usually not predictable. They can be higher in some years and lower in others. This causes the value of the company to fluctuate from year to year. If you bought the stock for $1,000 and sell it after five years, your stock could sell for more than $1,500, less than $500 or anything in between.

Year	1	2	3	4	5
Price	-$1,000				?
Dividends	?	?	?	?	?

However, over the long term, studies have shown conclusively that stocks have the best earnings potential of any major investment.

Owning a bond

Suppose Mikey Shoes obtains money by borrowing instead of by issuing shares. The company can do so by selling (or issuing) a bond. In this case, an investor buys the bond and the money is loaned to the company for a specified period of time. He is promised a regular interest payment every year. And the amount initially borrowed is returned to the investor at the end of the period.

For example, suppose Mikey Shoes sells a five-year bond that pays a rate of interest of 5 percent. This means if you buy $1,000 of bonds (thereby lending $1,000 to Mikey Shoes), the company will pay you interest of $50 a year for five years. At the end of five years, your $1,000 is returned to you. With a bond investment, you will know exactly how much money you will receive from the start of your investment. For this reason, bonds are generally safer than stocks.

Year	1	2	3	4	5
Price	-$1,000				$1,000
Dividends	$50	$50	$50	$50	$50

Starting to invest

In Singapore, persons as young as eighteen can start trading stocks and bonds listed on the Singapore Exchange. Many parents would probably feel uneasy about their teenage children having their own trading accounts—without requiring parental authorisation to trade. Scary? Yes but you can guide them.

There are safe bets that your child can consider and begin with and you can help them make their first investment. Here are a few ideas:

- *Buy stocks of companies your child likes.* This could be companies like Apple and Nike.
- *Invest in unit trusts.* In a unit trust investment, a group of investors come together to invest only in certain stocks and bonds. For example, they may focus on China stocks, global bonds or companies that manufacture luxury goods. In Singapore, you can invest by opening a Personal Account with a unit trust distributor like Fundsupermart. The minimum age to open a Personal Account is eighteen. Once you have a Personal Account and you want a separate portfolio for your twelve-year-old who is too young to have his own Personal Account, you can tag a Beneficiary Account to your Personal Account. The Personal-Beneficiary Accounts will be operated by you only but your child will be able to see his own investments in his very own portfolio.
- *Buy an exchange-traded fund (ETF).* An ETF allows you to buy a small piece of the Singapore economy. Here's how it works. It is a type of fund that tracks the movement of a stock index such as the Straits Times Index (STI). The STI consists of a basket of the thirty-largest companies listed on the SGX. These companies belong to industries that together provide a good benchmark of the Singapore economy. This means that if the Singapore economy is going through a rough patch, then the STI would reflect a downward trend. You can buy an STI ETF on the SGX. The minimum age to open a trading account is eighteen.

Becoming successful in investing

Keep these three ideas in mind:

- *Walk the talk.* If you preach savings and carefulness while you borrow and splurge, your kids will notice. If you live sparingly and show your children how to delay gratification, they will bring that approach to their investing. John Bogle, the legendary founder of Vanguard believes that you don't need to talk about investing that much to kids. Kids are really smart and observant. You live up to their expectations, or you don't. So walk the talk.

- *Keep learning.* Investing means putting your money to work for you so that you don't have to take a second job or work overtime frequently to increase your earnings. That is why it is important to learn about investing throughout our lives and to keep alive the conversations about investing with your children. Books written by successful investors such as Warren Buffett and Peter Lynch always provide inspiration and great lessons.

- *Keep things simple.* Don't flood your kids with Wall Street lingo. Just explain that owning a share of stock is like owning a piece of a company whose goods they like or whose stores they buy from. Kids aren't so much interested in hearing terms like diversification or market capitalisation. They are more likely to ask, "How can I buy a stock?" or "How much is my investment now worth?"

Adam says

I do my best to teach my children the concepts of earning income, spending and investing by playing board games like 'Monopoly', 'The Game of Life' and 'Cash Flow'. By playing with them, you can observe their decision-making habits when it comes to handling money and find a lot of opportunities to teach them concepts like buying low and selling high and investing in assets to collect future passive income. These are priceless life lessons that can be taught in a fun way that bonds the whole family.

What kids learn by earning money from investing

The idea behind investing is that money should be put to good use. Left idle, it can lose its value through inflation. There are many instruments to invest in, such as stocks, bonds, unit trusts and ETFs, and they don't require a large sum of money to start.

Investing however can be risky where losses can devastate even experienced investors. That is why learning about how investing works is critical not only for your children but also for yourself. Your children need to be guided by you and you can always learn more about how to invest carefully with your money especially when you are steadily moving towards retirement.

Investing allows your children to add extra income to their allowance. When you start your children on investing early in their lives, the experience will be invaluable to your family's financial future.

Quiz

1. **You want sixteen-year-old Jonathan to work during his holidays instead of hanging out at the mall and playing video games all day long. He's refused even though he would like more money for spending. You:**
    a. Find out what he might like to do if he had to work.
    b. Cut back on his allowance to force him to work and earn.
    c. Force him to find a job because he is wasting time during his holidays.
    d. Let him be and not force the issue. He has his whole life to work anyway.

(a) 3 (b) 1 (c) 1 (d) 2
It would be rare to find anyone who doesn't like to work, feel productive and earn money in the process. You need to help Jonathan find out what he likes to do for work. If he likes meeting people at the mall and talking about video games perhaps he may enjoy a retail job in an electronics shop. Never cut back on his allowance because having or not having a holiday job should not impact on something regular like an allowance. Instead of forcing him to get a job, try asking him to do extra chores at home to earn some money.

2. **Your fifteen-year-old Stephanie got a part-time job at a fast food restaurant. The job requires her to be on duty one weekend day every week even during the school term. She enjoys the work and money so much that she wants to work more and more hours. You:**
    a. Tell her to stop working until she learns what her priorities are.
    b. Put a limit to the number of hours because otherwise her school work will be affected.

c. Let her do so as long as she is completing her school
    work and getting enough rest.
d. Put a limit to the number of hours and pay her more
    allowance to make up any difference.

(a) 1 (b) 3 (c) 2 (d) 2
*Working during the school term is an excellent opportunity to
pick up skills, experience and extra pocket money. But like in
everything else, a balance must be struck between school and
work. Your child and you have to agree that she should not be
working more than a certain number of hours a week. She must
be getting her school work done and getting enough rest. Her
allowance should not be tampered with just because she wants
more money. The allowance is based on a planned, predictable
budget.*

3. **Your twelve-year-old Sally has been cleaning your
    neighbour's kitchen for extra pocket money. You hear from
    your neighbour that Sally does not do a good job with the
    cleaning and he has to clean up after Sally. You:**
    a. Punish Sally by giving her extra chores in the house.
    b. Speak to your neighbour about how Sally can improve.
    c. Tell your neighbour that Sally is just a kid and not to be
        so critical.
    d. Find out why Sally is not doing a good job. Perhaps she is
        just not good at cleaning.

(a) 1 (b) 3 (c) 1 (d) 3
*Getting a job done well requires Sally to know what she is doing
right or wrong, and for you to understand your neighbour's
expectations. Like in any job in the adult world, an understanding
between the two parties is necessary and it may even help to
have that understanding written as a simple agreement that's*

signed by your neighbour and Sally. You should also find out if Sally may be more suited to another task. We know some kids who love to clean indoors and some others who prefer physical work outdoors. Try to match your kid's ability and interest to the job but keep in mind that sometimes we cannot be completely picky when we need to earn a living.

4. **You create a Beneficiary Account for your son Terry but he has no interest in investing whatsoever. You bought shares in McDonald's and he says it is boring. You:**
   a.   Find out why Terry is not interested.
   b.   Offer to match what he puts into the account from his savings.
   c.   Close the account and find another time to broach the subject to Terry.
   d.   Continue to invest yourself and find occasions to tell Terry how your investments are doing.

(a) 3 (b) 3 (c) 2 (d) 3

Making your money work for you is what we believe separates those who have barely enough from those who have more than sufficient. Unless your child has the traits of a high-flying entrepreneur, chances are that he will be working for someone one day and earning a fixed salary. Investing your money is an important skill you need to use throughout your life so find out what it is that Terry doesn't like. If it's the reams and reams of numbers that turn him off then visit McDonald's with him to see how as a shareholder, your son is earning money whenever a burger or a sundae is sold. Encourage him to put some of his allowance into the account as long-term savings. Match what he puts in so he can see his portfolio doubling each time. You need to eat what you cook. Hence you need to be investing yourself and learning to keep two, three or four steps ahead of your kids.

5. **Justin wants to learn more about investing. He asks you questions that you struggle to answer. You:**
   a. Tell him that his priority is his school work.
   b. Start to invest yourself in order to learn and earn.
   c. Send Justin for an investing class to get his questions answered.
   d. Enroll yourself into an investing class and read books on investing.

(a) 1 (b) 3 (c) 3 (d) 3
Wealth is created in your spare time. Look at Mark Zuckerberg. He created Facebook in his spare time while in his dormitory at Harvard University. School should not be only about school. If your kid is asking tough questions then it's an opportunity for you to learn along. Send him to classes. Send yourself to classes. Read widely and make investments yourself. The amount you invest does not have to be large but you need to keep up with the monthly statements, the price of your investments, news about the companies you've invested in and enjoying the whole investing process. The more you know the more you enjoy and this will increase your family's chances of being successful investors.

CHAPTER 8
GRATITUDE

The less you want, the more you love.

"Gratefulness is the key to a happy life that we hold in our hands, because if we are not grateful, then no matter how much we have we will not be happy—because we will always want to have something else or something more."

—DAVID STEINDL-RAST

(MEMBER OF THE BENEDICTINE ORDER OF CATHOLIC MONKS)

HOW KIDS SHOW UNGRATEFULNESS

From a hapless father

Brian was obsessed with getting a Transformers action figure. Whenever we walked past a toy store, he would start his pleading. Convinced that nothing would make him happier than a Transformer, I broke down and bought him the most expensive version on the market for Christmas.

"He will be so thankful when he opens this gift," I told myself. And yes, Brian was thrilled—for about a week. Then, we noticed the Transformer spent most of its time in his closet, as Brian begged for other toys—a train set, a water gun, a basketball.

"You'd think he'd be grateful for what he has," I complained to my wife. "The more we give him, the less he appreciates it."

Does the following account sound familiar? Kids sometimes seem to have a knack for showing ungratefulness.

- "Mum, I need help with my homework—NOW."
- "That looks disgusting. I'm not eating it."
- "I'm not going to visit Grandpa. You can't make me."

GRATITUDE BRINGS JOY

Spiritual teacher Eileen Caddy said, "Gratitude helps you to grow and expand; gratitude brings joy and laughter into your life and into the lives of all those around you." By learning gratitude, kids:

- Become more sensitive to the feelings of others, develop empathy and other life skills.
- Look outside their one-person universe and understand that their parents and other people do things for them—prepare dinner, buy toys, give hugs.

But gratitude is a tricky concept to teach young kids. At that young age they are by nature self-centred because they haven't quite developed the sense of empathy.

No one is born grateful. Recognising that someone has gone out of the way for you is not a natural behaviour for children—it must be taught and it must be learnt.

I've got something even better than anti-depressants. Why not take this paper and write down all the things you are grateful for.

TEACHING GRATITUDE

Children who aren't taught to be grateful end up feeling entitled. They are perpetually disappointed and unhappy. Moments of thankfulness open our hearts to joy, fill us with peace, connect us to those around us. They help us feel blessed.

We want to share a few ways on how to teach gratitude. But before that, here's a brief note on how *not* to teach it.

How *not* to teach gratefulness

Teaching your children to say 'thank you' is only half the battle. The other half is to teach them to be thankful. Sometimes though, when we try to teach our children thankfulness, we go about it in surprisingly negative ways. For example:

- We force gratefulness on them: "You ought to be grateful for all the clothes you have." This is no different from saying, "stop whining."

- We use guilt on them: "Dear God, we are grateful for all the things we have, because we know that there are so many other children who have no parents and no toys and no nice home." This is the same as saying, "Maybe you don't deserve what you have." This is likely to instil guilt rather than gratitude.

Make it a point to tell your children about the good things at work as part of your daily conversations with them. When you reinforce an idea frequently, it's more likely to stick. Speak positively about the things you have.

- "We're so lucky to have a good cat like Sam!"
- "Isn't the sound of rain so soothing?"
- "I'm so happy when you listen!"

Have kids do chores and let them complete them

Once you give your child a chore, let her complete the chore even if it's agonising to watch her take forever to clear the table or she is making a mess mixing the pancake batter.

The temptation is to step in and do it yourself. Don't. The more you do for them, the less they appreciate your efforts. (Don't you feel more empathy for people who wash dishes when you wash dishes yourself?)

By participating in simple household chores, kids realise that all these things take effort.

Keon says

I watched the sixties movie *Pollyanna* many times as a child and it never fails with that pick-me-up feeling. In the movie, Pollyanna is a young orphan who goes to live with her wealthy Aunt Polly. Pollyanna plays "The Glad Game" everyday, an optimistic attitude she learnt from her father. The game is about finding something to be glad about in every situation. One Christmas, Pollyanna, who was hoping for a doll as a gift, found only a pair of crutches inside. Making up the game on the spot, Pollyanna said she was glad about the crutches because "we don't need them!"

If you are looking for a modern day version, try *Forrest Gump*. When Alibaba founder Jack Ma, the richest man in China, is feeling down, he looks to Forrest Gump for inspiration. He's watched the Tom Hanks movie over ten times. Work gratitude into your daily conversations.

Teach them to see the good in someone they don't like

This is tough we know. Try telling this to yourself when you have persons that you just cannot deal with, like difficult co-workers. Many people don't like confrontations, and simply avoid it.

Your child needs to learn to do this too. Have her write down all the positive qualities of the person that's bugging her. Such positiveness will teach her that she has to deal with difficult people, and when she does so, she will enhance her own life and personal growth immensely.

For birthdays and special occasions, give 'parent coupons'

Jaclyn did well on her school test. Rather than give her a gift, give her a parent coupon. The coupon could be for an extra story at bedtime, cycling by the beach, a day at the zoo.

Also encourage your children to give you kid coupons for things they will do for you, such as a day without fighting, taking a bath without whining, cleaning their room with a smile—anything that will make you happy.

Adam says

There are many ways in which we instil the sense of gratitude in our children. As part of their daily prayer ritual, my children are led in prayer to thank God for their blessings as well as to bless the people in their lives. When it's a family member's birthday, our children make their own cards and write down all the thanks and appreciation they have for Grandpa, Grandma and even the nanny. We often bring them along to volunteer at orphanages, children's homes (overseas as well) and the temples where they get to experience how difficult life is for the less fortunate who have so much less than they have. It seems to have worked as my children do not demand toys from us and will not throw a tantrum if we refuse to buy them something. They will happily agree with us and are grateful for what they have been given.

RECEIVING COMPLIMENTS WITH GRATITUDE

While people generally enjoy offering positive feedback, others find it difficult to be on the receiving end of genuine compliments. Have you ever praised your child: "Gary, you really did good with your school project. You have such an eye for art."

Only to hear something like: "Oh Dad, it's no big deal. Just another school project."

Learning to receive meaningful praise boosts a child's self-esteem and strengthens good behaviour. What are some Do's and Don'ts to teaching your child to receive praise?

The DO's of receiving praise

Accept compliments with a simple "Thank you." Let the person know that you appreciate the compliment: "Thank you for saying that. I worked really hard on this art project."

Look the person in the eye with a friendly smile when you acknowledge the compliment. Teach kids that without this, the words of appreciation may not seem sincere.

The DON'Ts of receiving praise

Don't brush off the compliment by disagreeing with it. If you are complimented on your golf game, do not say, "I totally messed up today—I usually score way more." You may think you are being humble, but a young person watching may think you are insulting the person who complimented you and could even make you look ungrateful.

Teach your child not to give the compliment away to someone else. Don't say, "Oh, I couldn't have done it without Ally." Be proud of your personal strengths and acknowledge the compliment with confidence!

Don't return the compliment like a boomerang. While it is always nice to compliment others, returning a compliment immediately often sounds insincere.

Quiz

1. **You just bought the most expensive Transformer toy for twelve-year-old Brian for Christmas. He plays with it for a week and is now clamouring for more Christmas presents. You:**
    a. Remind him how much he has compared with poor kids.
    b. Tell him that if he wants more toys, he will have to save for them.
    c. Take the Transformer toy back until he learns to be more grateful.
    d. Restrict the number of toys he gets during special occasions like Christmas.

    (a) 1 (b) 3 (c) 1 (d) 3
    Teaching gratitude to Brian would be futile if he usually gets more than he needs in terms of toys, money and snacks. Restricting the number of toys he can receive teaches him to appreciate what he already has and not to clamour for what other kids have. If there are specific toys that he wants that's not on the birthday list, then he needs to save for it through his allowance. Telling him how lucky he is compared with other kids is taking him on an unnecessary guilt trip. Taking the toy back is not a good idea when it had already been promised to him. It is also a sign that you may have failed to control his appetite by staying with the budget plan.

2. **Denise receives a B+ on her science test, which is an improvement from her previous grade of B. You praise her "Good job Denise," and she replies, "Nah, it's not good enough until it's an A." You:**
    a. Reserve the compliment only when she receives an A.
    b. Teach her to return the compliment to you so that it's fair.

c. Instruct her to say "thank you" to accept the compliment.

d. Tell her that people may not want to praise her if she refuses compliments.

(a) 1 (b) 1 (c) 3 (d) 3

Giving a compliment to someone and having it rejected is not only insulting and insincere but annoying. It's an even worse feeling for you when the person you are giving the compliment to received a higher grade than you did. Saying thank you with a sincere thankfulness is a basic courtesy that every child (and adult) must have. And never return the compliment right away as it shows insincerity. After all why didn't you initiate the compliment in the first place?

3. **Your sixteen-year-old Bessie has turned into an ungrateful teenager. She does little around the house, you spend most of your money providing for her and she doesn't seem to appreciate anything you do. You:**

a. Walk away when she is disrespectful towards you.

b. Make her in charge of fixing dinner one night a week.

c. Remove privileges if she doesn't help around the house.

d. Have her accompany you to the orphanage every month.

(a) 3 (b) 3 (c) 3 (d) 3

Your ungrateful child was not born; she was created by your over-indulgence. Fortunately your ungrateful teenager can be reformed and each of the four choices work. Parents can require their teenage children to make meaningful contributions to the family and to the community. If the chicken is burnt while fixing dinner, don't bail her out by ordering pizza. There are consequences that adults face in real life that teenagers will have to deal with one day and being over-protective is neglecting your child's development. Volunteering time at the orphanage is a wonderful way to help others and let your child make a difference in other people's lives. Over time she will learn that others who have far less than she does can still get on in life and be happy. But do make sure it's a regular activity and not just a tradition to 'make the family feel good' about themselves.

SUMMARY

A growing body of research suggests that maintaining an attitude of gratitude can improve psychological, emotional and physical well-being.[10]

Adults and children who frequently feel grateful have more energy, more optimism, more friends and more happiness than those who do not. They earn more money, sleep more soundly, exercise more regularly and have greater resistance to illnesses.

Kids benefit similarly. Kids who feel grateful tend to be less materialistic, get better grades, set higher goals, and feel more satisfied with their friends, families and schools than those who don't.

---

10   For more information, read Melinda Beck, "Thank You. No, Thank You," *The Wall Street Journal*, 23 Nov 2010.

CHAPTER 9
COLLEGE

SAVING AND PREPARING FOR COLLEGE

Having a university degree is widely seen as key to career success and increasing your child's income potential. Does that mean parents have to pay for it?

We all know the cost of a university education can run into hundreds of thousands of dollars.

	Singapore	Australia	UK	US
2014	$32,640	$208,000	$203,200	$290,800
Inflation (living expenses)	1%	2.1%	3%	2.3%
Inflation (education)	6%	8%	8%	6%
2024	$58,453	$367,399	$379,687	$520,778

Adapted from www.dbs.com.sg/personal/insurance/edusmart/fnacalculator.page

Don't let these numbers scare you into inaction. Some of your child's education can be paid for through scholarships and student loans. It's possible to save the rest if you start early, contribute regularly and invest wisely.

Investing for college

Saving for your children's college education through a savings account is not a good idea when the rate of college inflation is two to three times the rate of inflation. To amass sufficient money to finance four years of college, you need to start early and also invest rather aggressively. Putting more into equities would be a good idea especially if there are ten years or more till your children enter college. Equities can be used synonymously with stocks. It is the more general term to signify ownership in companies or other assets like real estate. Speak to a financial planner and let him help you to plan.

At the financial advisor's office...

I take it that you are not fond of equities.

Don't just park your money in a fund or two and leave it. Review the performance of the funds at least annually. When your child is five years from starting college, begin to shift your money into more bond funds, reducing your exposure to market ups and downs.

Then two to four years before your child is due to start college, cash in enough stocks and bonds to pay for the first two years, and put it somewhere safe and accessible, like a money market fund or fixed deposit. If you wait until just before you need the money, you may be forced to take it out at a time when the market is down, and you won't have the time to recover the losses.

Paying for college

Some parents will do anything to pay fully for their kid's college education even if it puts their future retirement in jeopardy. But paying fully is not possible for many parents. Next to your home, a college education for your child is probably the most expensive single item you'll ever pay for. Unless you have sufficient funds set aside for your children and your retirement, you will have to make some important choices regarding funding your child's college education.

Keon says

My parents paid fully for my first degree in the US. They didn't get the chance to go to college themselves and wanted to make sure that I didn't have to worry about having to work part-time to pay for my expenses. They sold the family home and moved into a smaller place so that I could study. Fortunately, that didn't stop me from working as a janitor, cleaning floors and toilets five days a week for three years. I am glad to have contributed to the cost of my own education.

Why parents should consider not paying fully

Here are three reasons why (even if you have the financial means):

- *You can take a loan for college but you cannot take a loan for retirement.* Paying fully could delay your retirement by five years or more. At the end of those five years, you may have drained your savings at a time when you are less employable. Remember that your child has the rest of his longer life to repay his loans.

- *Your child will work harder.* If he knows that the cost of college is his responsibility, he will be more conscientious about studying because good grades can result in more academic scholarship opportunities.

- *It promotes responsibility at an earlier age.* Instead of turning 26 and realising that it's time to get 'responsible' your kid will realise this at eighteen. There are many cases of adult children in their mid-twenties who still live at home and maintain the mindset of teenagers.

Splitting the college bill

For a start, we suggest that you don't aim to pay the entire bill. If you can come up with a third of the money your kids need for college before they go, you are doing a good job.

- Think about perhaps paying another third out of your future cash flow.
- And have them borrow the final third.

Meanwhile, make sure that you are saving and investing for your own retirement. Then work on three things—salary increases, bonuses and windfalls. Set aside a good portion of these irregular cash flows for your children and your retirement.

Keon Says

When Sarah was born, a financial planner convinced me to set aside $250 every month in an endowment fund for her. Although I thought that it was too early to do so, I am glad that I signed up. When she turned eighteen, the endowment matured and paid for nearly two years of college.

Adam says

From a young age, my wife and I have done our best to teach our children to be independent. Despite having two maids in our employment, we insist that our children make their beds, wash the dishes, clean their shoes and help lay the table for dinner. When they make a mess, they are expected to clean it up themselves. This form of upbringing has made them a lot more mature, independent and confident, as compared to other children their age.

As parents, we have been setting aside a savings and investment plan so that there is a reasonable amount set aside for college in the future. We do not believe in spending a few hundred thousand dollars sending our children overseas to study. With subsidies at local universities, it is more prudent for them to study locally and if they would like to study overseas, they will have to work hard to earn themselves a scholarship.

I believe that our children should pay for part of their college tuition as well as their own living expenses by taking on part-time jobs in college. The first reason is that they will really value the cost of education and take it a lot more seriously. More importantly, the experience they will get from working will be far more valuable in their future careers than what they learn academically in the classrooms.

Children saving for their own college

Here are some simple strategies to consider to help you grow your children's education savings accounts:

- *Open a dedicated long-term savings and an investment account for your child from as soon as it is possible.* A child as young as seven years of age can open a bank account for savings. Your child can also have a Fundsupermart Beneficiary account to hold investments at any age as long as it's tagged to a Personal account holder who is at least eighteen years old.

- *Consider automatic contributions from your monthly pay cheque.* Automating the process makes it feel less painful. Also ask family members and friends to contribute to your child's savings plan in place of gifts. Make sure your child writes a nice thank you note. Such notes are always appreciated!
- *Encourage your kids to save for their college as well.* Match what they contribute up to a certain percentage.
- *Regularly show them the account statements to get them excited about their own money.* Besides savings, teach them different investment options and show them how they will be able to pay for college when the time comes. For investment options, do seriously think about getting a financial planner to help you. Such planners are able to help plan your financial contributions to match your long-term objectives.

I am always thrilled to learn that kids as young as six or eight can actually appreciate events that take place ten or even twenty years in the future. That's because the internet and social media today are creating kids who are far more exposed to the world. They are growing up much faster than we did when we were young. So get them involved in their college planning as soon as they are in primary school.

THREE IMPORTANT SKILLS FOR YOUR KIDS BEFORE THEY ENTER COLLEGE

Budgeting

Budgeting should not be new to your kids by the time they go to college. Have them itemise their expected expenses for their first and second years. Universities usually give estimates of what a student's budget looks like for housing, food, tuition, transportation, insurance, entertainment and clothing. Let them work out a proper budget before dispensing any money. Money is limited and they have to plan how their money should be used.

Learning to cook

To live well, we have to eat well, and the only way to eat well is to learn to cook. Send your kids to cooking school. Include in your college budget a good set of utensils, pots and pans. Take them grocery shopping and have them learn to stock the refrigerator

Steps for Roasting Chicken
1. Season chicken
2. Burn chicken
3. Call pizza delivery

with fruits, vegetables and other healthy snacks and foods. Make them cook you a meal every now and then—and you better eat their cooked food.

All these experiences will help your kids, because college is the first time they are away from you and the first time they have to be self-sufficient for their meals. They may have meal plans and the school cafeteria, but with irregular and late hours, healthy food is not always available.

Keon says

Like other parents, I started preparing Sarah with life and critical skills years before she entered the University of Arizona in 2012. She went to a Blue Ribbon high school, played the viola in a youth orchestra and learnt to speak basic Chinese and French. But we left out one thing—we didn't teach her how to cook. She put on over nine kilograms in the first six months of college from microwave dinners, late night greasy burgers and Chinese take-out.

Learning to live with roommates

College may be his first time sharing his living space with people he only recently met. While having a roommate has its challenges, it is also a great part of his college experience.

While your kid does not seem to have problems meeting new friends, it is good to give him some preparation before he leaves home to live with near-perfect strangers. Here are some tips laid out by college housing officials.[11]

* *Be clear from the beginning.* If your kid is a neat freak or sleeps after 2am, he should let his roommates know about his little quirks and preferences. Communicating these helps to eliminate small problems before they become big problems.

---

11 Brian Burnsed, "Five Tips to Getting Along With Your Roommate", *US News*, 13 August 2010, www.usnews.com.

- *They don't have to be best friends.* Your kid may meet roommates with whom they form lifelong friendships but be aware that it's not the norm. The only expectation your kid should have of his roommates is that they respect him and his living space. Anything beyond that is a gift.
- *Set rules.* Tell your kid to consider having a frank conversation with his roommates over the first few days to set some rules. Whether it is about cleaning the room, listening to music or having friends over, it is important for roommates to know what each other are uncomfortable with.

Your kid is a near-stranger to his roommates too and they will be doing their best to blend in and adjust as well. Thankfully, roommates generally want to get along in order to get going with what really matters—having an enjoyable college experience and graduating from college.

Keon says

Before I left to study in the US, I was the king of my own room. Never would I have imagined that in the four years of undergraduate studies, I would stay with room mates from Malaysia, Persia, Pakistan, America, Vietnam, Spain, Nigeria, Puerto Rico, Hawaii and Taiwan. It was both an amazing and frustrating experience. If I were to do it all over again, I would at least surf the internet to understand about their countries and cultures, or even pick up a few of their favourite phrases.

Quiz

1. **Congratulations, your boy is going to college in a year and you have saved up enough money to go to a local university. You:**
   a. Have him borrow one-third.
   b. Pay 100 percent of his fees and board.
   c. Encourage him to get a campus job.
   d. Do not pay 100 percent if he wants to go overseas.

   (a) 3 (b) 2 (c) 3 (d) 3
   It is always good to have your child pay something towards college even if you can afford it. If you really do want to pay fully then a good compromise is to do so only for local courses but if he wants to go overseas, then he'll have to foot part of the bill. Whether he studies locally or abroad, encourage him to have a campus job. He'll meet more people and learn valuable work skills.

2. **You have saved for Jamie's college and you just learnt she won a $50,000 scholarship. You:**
   a. Let Jamie have $10,000 to use anyway she likes.
   b. Take $3,000 from her college fund for a holiday.
   c. Keep the money to help Jamie buy her first home.
   d. Transfer some of her college funds into your own retirement fund.

   (a) 2 (b) 2 (c) 3 (d) 3
   Your child getting some scholarship money is like winning the lottery. Don't let the money fritter away although it's ok to enjoy a part of it. You might take a small amount as a reward for Jamie although $10,000 is a bit much. You might even dip into her college fund to go on a holiday. After all, you have worked hard to save for so many years and $3,000 seems like a reasonable amount for a one-time splurge. We like the idea of using some of the extra money to encourage her to own a home sooner than later because putting your own roof over your head provides stability and financial peace of mind.

3. **Gillian has had her own room since five and she's not looking forward to college where she has to be in a shared room. You:**
   a. Look for student housing that offers single rooms.
   b. Have her stay at home if she's going to a local university.
   c. Tell her she has no choice but to learn to stay with others.
   d. Send her to a girl's camp or Outward Bound to prepare her.

(a) 1 (b) 1 (c) 3 (d) 3

It would be a grave mistake to keep Gillian safe and secure in her own room. She will not only miss out on making friends but also develop anti-social habits. Send her to camp for a week or two where you might find twenty girls staying together in one room. Tell her that sharing a room with others is fun but prepare her on how to deal with roommates.

4. **Nathan is going to college in a few years time and you have enough only for the first year. You:**
   a. Pay from your future salary.
   b. Work extra hard at your job to save more.
   c. Prepare to take some money from your retirement funds.
   d. Tell Nathan that he has to get a loan for some of his college costs.

(a) 3 (b) 1 (c) 1 (d) 3

Plan on using your future salary to help pay. Remind Nathan that he has to co-pay through a loan. Never put your retirement plan on the back burner. If you do, you may not have enough time left to rebuild your retirement funds after Nathan graduates.

SUMMARY

Your children will become young adults before you know it. While home provided creature comforts their whole young life, college means leaving those home comforts to live with near-perfect strangers sometimes in a foreign land.

What's more, college is not cheap. If you are planning to send your kid to college in a decade's time, you will need to consider a college fund of around half a million dollars. Fund it but don't fund it fully. Never neglect your own retirement savings.

CHAPTER 10
PLANNING FOR THE UNEXPECTED

We experience all kinds of surprises and unexpected events every day. Most of these happenings have minor impact, but sometimes, they can be significant events of an unpleasant, life-changing nature, causing difficulties and stress for the family. You can plan for the unexpected. Acknowledge the fact that surprises and unexpected events are part of life. When you accept this fact and have a plan in place in case the unexpected happens, it will be easier to deal with whatever happens in life.

In the movie *Big Fish*, a young Edward (the male lead) and his friends meet a local witch who has a glass eye that reveals the eventual death of anyone who looks into it. Edward sees how he will die, and decides that he can hence live a life of adventure, risk and meaning because he knows he will survive everything in between.

In this chapter, we look at two major unexpected events and how to help kids cope—divorce and financial emergencies. And in the next chapter, we look at a third—how to help kids cope with the death of a parent and planning a legacy for them.

DEALING WITH DIVORCE

Divorce rates are very high today. While the statistics are reported regularly on the number of divorces per thousand people in any given year in Singapore, the more scary number is the probability of divorce during the years after a couple gets married. According to the Singapore Department of Statistics, around seven people out of every thousand married residents aged twenty and over divorced in 2012. In England and Wales, 42 percent of marriages end in divorce.[12]

Even more frightening is if your parents are divorced, you're at least 40 percent more likely to get divorced than if they weren't. In

---

12   "What percentage of marriages end in divorce?" Office for National Statistics,
     9 February 2013, www.ons.gov.uk.

other words, your children are more likely to divorce because you were divorced.[13]

And in most cases, divorces are not peaceful, amicable affairs. Veteran family lawyer Ellen Lee has handled over 2,000 divorce cases in 33 years. Over that time, she had fewer than ten cases where the couples parted on terms that were cordial and not acrimonious.[14]

Divorce mediation

It is common that the biggest victims of divorce are not the spouses but the children. If you and your spouse are headed towards a divorce, give mediation a try. Mediation is about you and your spouse meeting a neutral third party to decide the terms of your own divorce and what is best for the both of you and most importantly, your children.

---

13 Nicholas H Wolfinger, *Understanding the Divorce Cycle*, Cambridge University Press, 2005.

14 Tham Yuen-C, "Ugly divorce cases nearly made me shun marriage," *The Straits Times*, 16 September 2014.

In some countries (like Singapore since September 2011), couples with children below twenty-one years have to participate in mandatory counselling and mediation if they have filed for divorce. These sessions are "carried out at the early stages of divorce proceedings to help parents deal with their emotions, understand and focus on the needs of their children and to help them in their parental roles post-divorce. In this way they can move forward instead of becoming entrenched in their disputes."[15]

Adam says

My wife and I both come from divorced families so we know how difficult it can be for children when their parents do not get along. The silver lining is that both my wife and I are committed to avoid the same mistakes that our parents made—not communicating openly and not working together in raising children. My father and mother had very different styles when it came to raising me. My mum gave me everything I wanted and spoilt me while my Dad was the complete opposite. He was very strict and insisted that I had to earn my own keep. Needless to say, their disagreements on how to raise me contributed to their fights.

Learning from this, I have come to realise that in a family (like in a company or country), there can only be one boss. While the directors (spouses) can debate over the best course of action, the boss must ultimately have the final say. Both parties must then respect the final decision. Once the decision is made, the directors must stand united in front of other people, especially in front of the children.

While I am the boss when it comes to managing the family finances, my wife is the appointed boss when it comes to managing the children's affairs. When we have disagreements over how to raise our children, my wife has the final say and I will support her fully on it. That has been the key to our successful marriage and the raising of our children.

---

15 "Child Focused Resolution Centre—Phase Two," *SubCourts News*, Issue 6, I June 2013, pp 8.

POST-DIVORCE REQUIRES PLANNING

Every couple lines up at the altar with every intention of living happily ever after but the unfortunate reality is that marriages have a high chance of ending in divorce. Parents need to learn that when a marriage ends, divorced parents still share a common interest in raising financially responsible kids. But new types of conflicts arise. Does this sound familiar?

> Paula just returned from a weekend with her Dad. She's wearing a pair of designer jeans, has a new mobile phone (the one she's been saving to buy) and is happily chattering about the movie she saw. Boy, am I mad!

Speak with one voice

There is one key principle to avoiding such lose-lose conflicts. Parents must cooperate with each other and speak with one voice to their children. These are some of the important lessons we have learnt from divorced parents.

- *You are not divorcing your kids.* Some kids may think they caused the divorce especially if they have ever heard you arguing about them. Look your child in the eye and let him know that he could not have caused the divorce.
- *Don't badmouth your ex.* If you have differences with your ex, discuss him in private and not openly around the kids.
- *Let your kids know there is no possibility of your getting back together.* The sooner your kids stop fantasising about Mum and Dad getting back together, the sooner they heal and adjust.
- *You are still a team.* You may be divorced as husband and wife but not as father and mother. Let your kids know that they are still the most important people in your lives.

Keon says

Sarah's mother and I are divorced but we have remained very good friends through the years. We decided right from the start that we would never quarrel in front of Sarah. When major decisions have to be made for Sarah's education or health matters, we always worked towards a common consensus. In the end, getting along is part of being the best mother and father team we could be to Sarah, even though we don't live together.

WHAT KIDS WANT

When divorce is a clear solution to a disastrous marriage, it's easier for the kids to understand. While we do not advocate divorce for many reasons, we would not strongly insist that two people should stay married "for the sake of the children." One 45-year-old mother whose parents divorced when she was in her twenties said, "I wish my parents got divorced when I was much younger. They didn't get along and had fights all the time. My childhood is filled with painful memories and guilt that I wish I could forget."

What children need from their parents

How do two people who have no need for each other raise a child? By being more sensitive to the child's needs rather than your own. This is what your child needs from you:

- I need both of you to stay involved in my life. Even if you don't live close by, please write letters, make phone calls, and ask me lots of questions about who I spend time with and what I like and don't like to do. When you don't stay involved in my life, I feel like I'm not important and that you don't really love me.
- Please stop fighting and work hard to get along with each other. Try to agree on matters related to me and my needs. When you fight about me, I think that I did something wrong and feel guilty.
- I want to love you both and enjoy the time that I spend with each of you. Please support me and the time that I spend with each of you. If you act jealous or upset, I feel like I need to take sides and love one parent more than the other.
- Please communicate directly with my other parent so that I don't have to send messages back and forth. I want you to talk with each other so that the messages are communicated the right way and so that I don't feel like I am going to mess up.
- When talking about my other parent, please say only nice things, or don't say anything at all. When you say mean, unkind things about my other parent, I feel like you are putting me down and expecting me to take your side.
- Please remember that I want both of you to be a part of my life. I count on my Mum and Dad to raise me, to teach me what is important, and to help me when I have problems.

Adapted from Kim Leon and Kelly Cole, *Helping Children Understand Divorce*, University of Missouri Extension, March 2014, http://extension.missouri.edu/p/GH6600

WORK OUT A PLAN

It is easier said than done, but you and your ex-spouse have to work out a plan. Whether you have things written in the divorce settlement or monthly pow-wows with your ex-spouse, you need to communicate regularly to allow for changes in your children's school needs, health and spending habits.

Recognise that as parents you need help yourself in managing your own stress and mental health. Have your own therapist on hand to help you or even a trained mediator who can help you both develop a solid parenting plan with your welfare and that of your children's in mind.

While divorce is hardly a pleasant matter for both parents and children, there is a lot that can be done to make sure post-divorce matters like bringing up your children and finances can be smooth and pleasant.

DEALING WITH FINANCIAL EMERGENCIES

There are moments in life that will shake things up for you. It may be getting a pink slip at work, receiving a positive pregnancy test when you were not trying, or becoming disabled or critically ill when you have been in the pink of health. When these big events occur, they will affect your financial future, and you will need to involve your family and kids to deal with your new financial reality.

The best way to handle these events is to have prepared for the unexpected in advance. Yes, it can be done.

Getting prepared

The first step for preparing for a financial emergency is to have a solid emergency fund in place. This should be about six months of your income. If you are single or if you have a family but only one income provider you may want to increase this to a year. This will provide security while you recover from an emergency. It is nice to know you have the money there while you are dealing with other issues such as a job loss, illness or anything that might affect your income.

Second, you need to have adequate life insurance for yourself and your spouse. The life insurance should provide enough money to live on after you pass away. If you have children, you should get enough that it can help pay the cost of their education and living expenses until they have finished school. It is vital that you have life insurance coverage if you have children.

Third, you should have adequate health insurance coverage, including for hospitalisation and critical illnesses. Many people gamble with not having health insurance coverage, because they feel that they are in good health and do not need it. Medical bills add up quickly and all it takes is one serious illness or accident, and you could find yourself deeply in debt without the health insurance.

You also need to have mortgage insurance for your home. If you have been paying a large part of the monthly mortgage, your loss of income from job loss, illness or death would be a severe blow to your surviving family members.

It happens only to others

Some of you are naturally thinking that it only happens to others and not to you. But do consider:

- You have an 80 percent chance of experiencing a disability before age 65 that will keep you out of work for 90 days or more.[16]
- You have a 90 percent chance of dying from a critical illness such as cancer, heart disease and pneumonia.[17]

---

16 Ron Lieber, "The Odds of a Disability Are Themselves Odd," *The New York Times*, 5 February 2010. In the article, the author finds that statistics on the probability of becoming disabled sometimes seem stretched, but he nevertheless suggests that disability insurance is a 'fine idea'.

17 *Principal Causes of Death*, Ministry of Health Singapore, www.moh.gov.sg.

• You are very likely to experience one or more involuntary job losses in your working life. Then depending on your age, it could take you as much as three to twelve months or even longer to find another job.[18]

When the unexpected happens

You can plan for the unexpected as best you can, but nothing can quite completely prepare you when the unexpected does actually happen. When it does:

• *Take stock.* Quickly have a handle on your finances. Tally up your monthly expenses and create a survival budget to get a sense of how long your savings can keep you afloat. If you've been a diligent insurance buyer, you will now be able to tap on this much needed source of cash. And if you've been a diligent saver, your emergency fund can be activated for use.

• *Get your family involved.* Your children don't have to understand the details of your job loss or your illness, but they do need to appreciate the importance of cutting back. Don't try to protect your children by not discussing finances or your health condition around them. In your time of need, a joint family effort can yield great results. You can put it in terms they can understand—like instead of ordering out pizza three times a week, maybe you only do it once. Or arranging a visitation schedule to make sure you have family members visiting you when you are ill.

• *Stay away from your retirement funds.* It is never wise to raid your retirement accounts. That money is for you to use in your old age. Once you take that money out, you can't put it back, unless you take it out as a loan, but then you will just be creating another monthly bill to pay.

---

18 Sara Rix, "Unemployed For The Long-Term: It doesn't seem to get any better", *Huffington Post*, 20 April 2014, www.huffingtonpost.com.

DEALING WITH DEATH

Thanks to better healthcare and improved diets today, many of us can expect to live till our eighties and even beyond. Such statistics however often lull us into the false sense that we expect to pass away only when we are eighty. And that by then, our children would have all grown up. But what if you are wrong? Have you ever thought about your own premature passing and how your children will deal with it?

One estimate reveals that one in 29 children aged five to sixteen has experienced the death of a parent or sibling.[19] This means that your children are themselves, or are with friends in school who are already suffering from bereavement. You can imagine the difficulty of coping as an adult but what about how children can cope? The deeper work of grieving is not in the weeks surrounding the funeral, but in the months and years that follow.

Talking to children about death

Children need to know the truth about death. Telling them that "Daddy has gone on a long trip" can leave them more frightened and confused. They may think that Daddy has left and deserted them.

Instead tell the plain facts—"Daddy has died and we believe he is in heaven. It is a wonderful place, but I will miss him very much. I do wish he could have stayed with us longer. He also wishes that he was with us longer as well." Help children to grieve and express their emotions about the loss. It is alright to let them see you cry.

Like us, children want to make sense of what happened and we can help them. Name the disease and tell them what to expect in the course of treatment even if it's serious and potentially life-ending like cancer or leukaemia. If there was an accident let them know what happened and what will happen next. The more prepared they are the less out of control they feel.

---

19   Shelley Gilbert, "Helping children to cope with the pain of a parent's death," *The Guardian*, 4 May 2013.

Keon says

When my father passed away in late 2014, Sarah was in the midst of preparing for her final exams in Arizona. She was very close to her Grandpa and I was afraid to tell her what happened. In fact I wanted to tell Sarah only after her exams. But Sarah's mother insisted that she has the right to know. Sarah took it badly and started to miss classes. We kept in touch by phone a few times a day and I explained every detail I could about what happened. When Sarah visits Singapore in summer, we will commemorate her Grandpa's passing. We will visit the columbarium every year, look at our favourite photos and share fond memories.

Even at my age I was not comfortable dealing with death, what more for a child. But 'protecting' Sarah would have been the wrong thing to do.

Not all children process death the same way

Children are unique in their understanding of death and dying, depending on their maturity, personality and whether they were close to the person who passed away.

- Up to preschool, children may perceive that adults are sad, but have no real understanding of the meaning of death. They may see death as reversible, thinking that mummy will wake up after a long sleep.

- At around ten, children start to understand that death is final and not reversible. They understand that if large planes crash, people will be killed.

- In their teenage years, most will now fully understand the meaning of death. Teens are particularly at risk at a time when they are dealing with puberty and the pressures of teenage life. It is good if they seek out friends and family for comfort. Be watchful if they become withdrawn and depressed. Prolonged grief is a sign that they need more careful attention at home and in school. Consider therapy as a way for them to share their feelings in a safe and neutral environment.

Children may process death differently depending on who passed away.

- *Death of a parent.* It is a traumatic event when a primary caregiver passes away and you cannot hide this from your child. If you are the surviving parent, you have to first deal with your own feelings of loss and be strong to help your child get back to a routine as soon as possible. Assure him that you are not going to leave. You must return to work to earn a living and you need to find someone to provide a caretaking role for a while—perhaps a nanny or grandparents. Most of all, you will need to spend more time with your children and help them adjust to their new life.
- *Death of a grandparent.* Children may not find it as overwhelming as the loss of a parent or a sibling. Children are able to understand that their grandparent is an older person, and when people get old, they often pass away.
- *Death of a sibling.* When a brother or a sister dies, the impact can be as traumatic as losing a parent, sometimes even more. A sibling may be the person your child is closest to. They played together and even shared a bedroom. Even though you will be overwhelmed with your own sadness, your other children will need your attention even more.

Some adults believe that children should be shielded from death. They keep children away from funerals. They try not to cry in front of their youngsters. They may make up stories in an attempt to protect children from pain ("Grandma had to go away for a long time; we won't see her for a while"). They may avoid all discussions of the deceased.

Despite the good intentions of these actions, they don't work and are counterproductive. As with most topics, communicating with children about death should be honest and direct. Children need to grieve as much as adults do. They need to be able to share their feelings and talk about how they are going to miss the person who has died. By school age they have already been exposed to death, even if only indirectly, by watching television or hearing about it from friends. Death should not be covered up and hidden.

To help your child, you need to feel comfortable with your own grief reaction over the death of a loved one. It is appropriate for your child to see you cry when you feel sad; he will take comfort knowing that you are expressing your feelings so openly. This will make it easier for him to do the same.

Quiz

1. **You have been working with twelve-year-old Eva to save for a new smart phone. She spends the weekend with your ex-husband and she comes home excitedly with a new smart phone, exactly the one she was saving for. You:**
    a. Take the phone and return it to your ex.
    b. Forbid Eva to visit your ex until he behaves.
    c. Speak to your ex to cooperate and work together with you.
    d. Let her keep the phone but make her pay for it from her savings.

(a) 1 (b) 1 (c) 3 (d) 3
The grand plan is that you and your ex will always be the father and mother to your child. Quarrelling and disagreeing with your previous spouse does no good for the upbringing of your child. It is damaging and selfish. Neither is it helpful to forbid Eva from visiting your ex because Eva needs to see her father. And she could even resent you for stopping the visits. You and your ex have to agree to cooperate and act as mature parents. He should

have asked you before buying the phone especially when it's an expensive item. One way to punish him is to return the phone to him but that would only raise the tension. You could let Eva keep the phone and deduct it from her savings. And even here, your ex has to know and support this idea.

CHAPTER 11

LEAVING A MEANINGFUL LEGACY

We are indeed blessed in these times. We live longer today than ever in history and economic growth has produced a large population of middle class families who can afford homes, refrigerators and cars. For example, Singapore is one of the wealthiest countries in the world (top-five according to several surveys) and our life expectancy is in the top-five (over 82 years). However greater wealth and a longer life expectancy have been accompanied by troubling social issues. We are seeing an increase in divorce rates, a greater incidence of mental incapacity and spoilt children squabbling over their inherited wealth.

The consequences of too much wealth for children can be serious and this is something parents need to worry about. Children who receive too much too quickly grow up feeling entitled and will suffer long-term effects of dependency, irresponsibility and poor relationship skills.

In this chapter, we look at what you can do if you already have a spoilt child in your home. Then we look at legacy planning— how you can create a plan to leave behind an inheritance to your loved ones that takes care of their financial needs, yet does not spoil them by giving them too much too quickly and ensuring that important family values can be passed down to future generations.

DEALING WITH SPOILT CHILDREN

If you are spoiling your children, you will know it. They're rude to you and other adults, they won't share with other children, and they will be bossy, always demanding to be the first in line.

Many parents are clueless about how to deal with their children when they are exhausted from work and stretched from running the household. It's easier to give in to their wailing kids than to discipline them. But parents be warned—spoiling your kids can have very troubling consequences.

When spoilt youngsters become teenagers, they are more prone to excessive self-absorption, lack of self-control, anxiety, and depression. If you give kids so much early on, they get to a point where they can't be satisfied with anything. So where do you start? Here are steps you can take to regain control:

- *Make a real commitment to stop spoiling your children.* You have to commit. If you do it halfway, kids will sense your hesitation and they will continue to control you.
- *Do what you say.* Just say the words and say what's going to happen and stick to it. You don't even have to yell.
- *Be tough and discipline them.* Avoid the trap of explaining why over regular matters like cleaning the room and bedtime. If going to bed on time is a problem, try no television for the next 24 hours.

Could grandparents be the biggest spoilers?

Today's grandparents are healthier and wealthier than ever, and they are notorious for their generosity.

Striking a balance

"After I had told my children they cannot have a video game console unless they saved for it, their grandparents arrived and presented them with one. I let my children accept the gift but I was not happy."

Grandparents and their adult children need to strike a balance between the satisfaction grandparents get from buying stuff for the kids, and the parents' right to say enough is enough.

Disciplining Grandpa and Grandma

You should tell your parents to feel free to be spontaneous with small gifts. Or if they are visiting, come with plans to do something together—watch a movie, bake cookies, have a picnic. Or if they insist on buying something, have their grandparents take them shopping with a fixed budget. This way, they control their spending as well as spend time together.

For big gifts, your parents need to consult you and they should be given only on special occasions like birthdays. If they give money, do not confiscate it. Let your kids spend a portion and save the rest.

KIDS WANT THEIR PARENTS TO BE PARENTS

Our primary role as parents is to prepare your child for how the world really works. In the real world, you don't always get what you want. You will be better able to deal with that as an adult if you've experienced it as a child.

Adam says

Like most couples, my wife and I have had the difficult task of laying down rules for our own parents and in-laws to follow. Indeed, our parents have been guilty on more than one occasion of spoiling the kids with gifts and letting them get away with anything. After a lot of heart-to-heart talks, they have agreed to follow our rules and not spoil the market. This way, our children know they cannot override our rules by going around our backs to Grandpa and Grandma.

To raise children well, it is so important for all adults to speak with one voice in front of the children and never give conflicting instructions. Any disagreements should always be resolved away from the children and it should always be respected that parents have the final say. After all, we are ultimately responsible for the kids.

One of the things that motivated me to work hard for myself and to never expect anything from my rich father was something he said to me when I was twelve. He said, "Son, I love you very much. But don't expect me to leave you with anything when I am gone. It is my money and I will spend it on myself and give what's left away to charity." He went on to say, ' You grew up in a very comfortable home (with the helpers and a swimming pool) and if you can afford to live well next time, do not expect me to bail you out. I will only give you love and advice but nothing more." Knowing that at the back of my mind that there was no safety net created in me the hunger and the urgency to build my own wealth to secure my future. So, that is the same message I am going to give my girls. Although I will probably leave part of my wealth to them when I die, they are never going to know about it. In their minds, they must be prepared that they will receive nothing from me. This will ensure that they do not grow up with a sense of entitlement.

WHAT IF YOU HAVE NO LEGACY PLAN?

Like sex, death is probably not considered appropriate dinner conversation with children. But they should be aware of how you plan to provide for them if something happens to you and your spouse. Some of these matters include your will, trust, insurance policies, financial documents and information on who will look after them if you are no longer around.

Suppose your net worth at death (NWAD) is $2 million. Now we're not talking about your net worth today but at death. If you are Singaporean, you are likely to own an HDB government apartment or a private condominium, have over five insurance policies and several investments and bank accounts. If you pass away today, your NWAD may easily be S$2 million or more.[20]

Now suppose you didn't have anything planned such as having a will written. Then if you pass away, your assets will be distributed according to the law in your country. If you are Singaporean, 50 percent would go to your spouse and 50 percent would be shared equally among your children.[21]

You should see two big problems with this. First, your assets would not be distributed according to your wishes—what if you wanted your parents to inherit something or you wanted your favourite charity to receive a sum of money? Second and very scary, your teenager could become an instant millionaire without having to work for it. Not writing a will is like giving your children the winning ticket on the lottery.

20 Whether you are from Singapore, Malaysia or Australia, a NWAD of $2 million is a commonly attainable threshold for many middle-class and mass affluent persons. For high-net-worth individuals (HNWIs), their NWAD is even higher and their population in Asia Pacific is growing faster than the rest of the world. Wealth reports from Cap Gemini consistently show the HNWI population in Asia Pacific growing by double-digit percentages every year. In 2013 for example, that growth was 17.3 percent..

21 This is based on Singapore's Intestate Succession Act (cap 146) for non-Muslims. Every country in the world or if you are Muslim have their own intestacy laws, which generally direct distributions to immediate family members.

Don't let your children win the lottery: It could be a curse

At sixteen, Callie Rogers became Britain's youngest lottery jackpot winner. She gave up her job and frittered most of her money on parties, drugs, cosmetic surgery, holidays and gifts. Instead of bringing happiness, her riches left her feeling so lonely and vulnerable that she attempted suicide. She said, "For so long I drifted with no aim."

Fortunately for Callie, she got out of her rut. Ten years later at age 26, Callie has only £2,000 left in the bank—but says she has never felt happier. She lives in a modest home today with her partner and son. She works two days a week as a carer for the elderly and is studying to be a nurse.

Taken from Eleanor Harding, "My £2m lotto win at 16 was a curse", *Daily Mail*, 15 July 2013, www.dailymail.co.uk

BASIC INSTRUMENTS IN YOUR LEGACY PLAN

A will and a trust are the most basic documents that you need to consider for your legacy plan.

How your will takes care of your children

Your will not only outlines what happens to your assets and who will execute your instructions in the will, it also lays out how you want your children taken care of until they are old enough to be on their own.

A will takes care of your children by answering the following questions:

- *Who is the executor?* The executor of the will is someone you trust to make sure that your affairs are handled according to your specific wishes upon your death.
- *Who is to be the guardian of your children?* If there is no will, the court decides who gets custody or guardianship of your children (if your spouse is no longer around).
- *How will your children be taken care of financially?* Are your assets and insurance sufficient for their maintenance and education?
- *How do you plan to divide the assets among your children and beneficiaries?* Do you want your children to receive all your money at once or do you want the payments spaced out?

After you write your will, review it every few years. Things change. You may buy a new home, have more children or have other assets to deal with. All these things need to be considered in updating your will.

Explaining your will to your kids

Explaining your mortality is not an easy topic to discuss with your child. It has to be moved along gently especially if your children are very young.

Keon says

If you are married and have children, and you don't write a will, your parents may not inherit anything if you pass away. For most people this is clearly not acceptable but that is the law in many countries. With a will, besides setting aside assets and money to your spouse and children, you can also gift assets to your parents, a charity, nieces and good friends. It is a grave mistake to not have this basic legal document in place.

The will can be explained to them as "A written plan that lays out how a child will be cared for if something happens to his parents."

Add that the plan will not be used until you are very old and your child has grown up. But the plan is there just in case there is an emergency.

CONSIDER A TRUST FOR DELAYED DISTRIBUTIONS

If your NWAD is at least a few hundred thousand dollars to a few million and you have young children, then you need to consider a trust. If you have a will that only makes immediate distributions upon death, consider the following situations:

- Your son could become an instant millionaire as young as 21. Having received his inheritance, he drops out of school and decides not to work the rest of his life.
- Your spouse could remarry and the assets you worked for could then be benefiting someone you hadn't planned on benefiting.

A trust is a special instrument that allows distributions to be held and delayed based on conditions you set today and can amend through the years. For example:

- Your son may receive a reasonable sum of $30,000 a year for maintenance. Upon graduation, he could be given a lump sum of $50,000. In order to continue benefiting from the trust, he has to hold down a proper job.
- Your spouse may benefit from the trust only for her own maintenance and medical needs, and not for other individuals.

Contrary to what many think, you do not need to be a millionaire to have a trust. You can put trust instructions in a will. For example you may set aside $200,000 for your daughter in the following way:

- "I give $20,000 to my daughter every year for ten years starting when she is at least 25 years old. She may use the money for whatever purpose she decides."

Such a trust is called a testamentary trust and is set up only upon death. Another type of trust is called a living trust, which is set up today while you are alive.

There are many features of wills and trusts that could fit your specific situation. You should speak to a practitioner in this area such as an estate planner or a lawyer.

GETTING AN INITIAL LEGACY PLAN TOGETHER

Here's an example to help you begin to pen down some thoughts about your own plan. You should focus on the planning issues and leave aside the technical and legal aspects. Focusing on the technical details right away could cause you to lose track of what you really need to do.

Get a piece of paper and pen

Divide a piece of blank A4-sized paper into four Quadrants as shown in the sample on the next page. It's already filled in with an example of Adam aged 45 and his family. His wife Betty is forty and his two children are ten and twelve.

Quadrant A—Specify your main beneficiaries

In Quadrant A, Adam's beneficiary tree is drawn up. The tree represents the people he wishes to benefit should he pass away. He and his wife have two children. Both his parents are still alive, and his wife's father has passed away.

Quadrant B—List down your assets

Next, specify what your assets are. How assets are owned is an important consideration for inheritance purposes. Your assets or what you own can be divided into two main groups—(a) immovables are assets that 'do not move' like homes, land and properties, while (b) movables are assets that can move like bank accounts, stocks, insurance policies, jewellery, bicycles and antiques. Assets can be owned solely, jointly (under joint tenancy or tenancy in common) or by an entity such as a company or a trust.

Most of what Adam owns is situated in Singapore although he has a bank account and an apartment both situated in the UK. Adam estimates that his NWAD is about S$3.2 million.

Quadrant C—Specify immediate gifts

Adam wishes to give S$200,000 in total to his parents should he pass away. That leaves S$3 million for his wife and two children. Of the remaining assets, Adam wishes to leave one-third each to his wife and children. Should Adam write a will to make these gifts immediately to them?

If he did and then he passes away in the next few years, his young children could become millionaires at a very young age.

Quadrant D—Specify delayed gifts

After speaking with an estate planner, Adam decides to delay the gifts to his children. Should he pass away and his children are still young, he wishes to entrust the S$1 million to a trustee. A trustee is a person or institution that would hold the money Adam left for his children for a specific period of time.

Adam wants the trustee to release money to his children only for maintenance, education and medical expenses up to S$10,000 a month. Then when his children each reach thirty, the remaining money can be given to them.

A SIMPLE LEGACY PLAN

A. YOUR BENEFICIARY TREE	B. YOUR ASSETS	

Mother Father   Mother
   | |
Husband   Wife
        \   /
      Son/Daughter
	Movables
	Singapore bank account
	UK bank account
	Investments
	Insurance
		Immovables
		Private condo
		apartment (UK)

C. IMMEDIATE GIFTS	**D. DELAYED GIFTS**	
To give $100,000 each to my father and mother immediately upon my passing	Primary objective: To benefit my children until each is thirty years of age. When to distribute: Only for maintenance, education and housing up to $10,000 a month.	

The above example is very simplified of course. In reality you may own overseas assets that are subject to inheritance and estate taxes, you may own property that is jointly owned or held under a company, or you may want to withhold money from your children should they fall into bankruptcy. You may also have bank loans or you have intentions to make gifts to several charities. These situations require more careful planning.

SUMMARY

If you have spoilt children, you can do something to reverse the process. You can be tough, make them involved in maintaining the household. Bear in mind that your children will suffer serious long-term effects if they continue their sense of entitlement into adulthood.

If you leave this world, you do not want your kids to inherit too much of your money too quickly. You may have brought your kids up well that they are careful with money. But you cannot control the people who may be hanging around them for the wrong reasons. Don't leave things to chance. Have a legacy plan in place that you can amend over the years. It will give you peace of mind that your money and values you want to uphold in your family will be transferred prudently to your loved ones when you are no longer around.

Quiz

1. **Ten-year-old Caleb is throwing a tantrum at the steak house. He wants to skip the main dish and go straight to dessert. You:**
   a. Continue eating and ignore his demands.
   b. Tell him you will remove TV privileges for one week.
   c. Give in to him as he's embarrassing the whole family.
   d. Walk out of the restaurant, skip the meal and go home.

(a) 3 (b) 3 (c) 1 (d) 2
If you allow Caleb to get his way, he is sure to try the same stunt with his friends, his cousins and grandparents. Then soon no one will want to hang around Caleb. Tell him you will remove his TV privileges and make sure you do so. Never make empty threats. Unless he is screaming and making a big scene, try continuing to eat and ignoring his demands. He needs to learn that in the real world he cannot have everything he wants. Walking out of

the restaurant means everyone goes home hungry. While this is drastic, Caleb needs to learn that his poor behaviour affects the whole family, not just him.

2. **Your net worth at death is about S$2 million consisting of your insurance policies, home, bank account and car. You wrote a simple will a few years ago to give half of your assets to your forty-year-old husband and the other half to your fourteen-year-old son. If this is your main instruction for distributing your assets, what are some potential issues with your will? Tick all that apply:**

   a. Guardianship of your son. In the event you and your husband pass away together at the same time.

   b. Benefiting a stranger. Your husband could inherit your assets, remarry and benefit someone else with your money.

   c. Ruining your child's life. Your son would receive his inheritance at 21 and he could decide to drop out of college and spend his inheritance wastefully. He may attract unsavory friends who are after his money.

   d. Other beneficiaries. You hadn't thought then about leaving something for your parents or for your favourite charity.

All these are issues that need to be dealt with if you are no longer around—the guardianship of your children, your spouse remarrying or your children squandering your wealth and wasting their lives away. Writing a simple will can sometimes be harmful to your family's financial future if it doesn't consider these and other issues. For many families, a trust needs to be considered too where you want the distribution of your assets to be subject to certain conditions. Make sure you review your estate plan every couple of years or when major events occur such as the birth of new children, when new assets are acquired or there is a death in the family.

ALSO BY ADAM KHOO

I AM GIFTED, SO ARE YOU!
ISBN 978 981 4561 48 8, S$30.75

Every student can achieve and excel if given the opportunity! This book will inspire legions of students to stretch and realise their potential. It tells the inspiring story of an underachieving 13-year-old's rise to become among the top 1% of students in the National niversity of Singapore, and earn a place on the Dean's list every consecutive year for outstanding academic achievements. Adam shares with readers the skills and success strategies of his personal journey, in simple and clear terms, with exercises to help train others in his techniques. It is the perfect book for students, parents, educators and anyone who wants to enhance his or her brainpower.

ALSO BY KEON CHEE

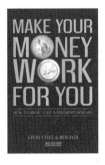

MAKE YOUR MONEY WORK FOR YOU
(3rd edition)
with Ben Fok
ISBN 978 981 4328 61 6, S$26.00

This book shows you how to invest in the simplest possible way. Whether you are a veteran or new to investing, you will find sensible advice about where you should invest your money—in traditional investments like stocks, bonds and unit trusts or non-traditional ones such as hedge funds, REITs and structured deposits.

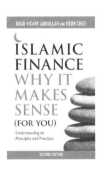

ISLAMIC FINANCE
(2nd edition)
with Daud Vicary Abdullah
ISBN 978 981 4408 22 6, S$27.00

In this second edition, the authors discuss three new topics: microfinance, the Ethical Company and Wealth Succession. As in the best selling first edition, published in 2010, this volume explains and updates how conventional financial products work—from mortgages and lease to trade finance and insurance — before delving into their Islamic versions. This book will help you make sense of Islamic finance on a broader scale.